Why Politics Can't Be
Freed From Religion

Blackwell Manifestos

In this new series major critics make timely interventions to address important concepts and subjects, including topics as diverse as, for example: Culture, Race, Religion, History, Society, Geography, Literature, Literary Theory, Shakespeare, Cinema, and Modernism. Written accessibly and with verve and spirit, these books follow no uniform prescription but set out to engage and challenge the broadest range of readers, from undergraduates to postgraduates, university teachers and general readers – all those, in short, interested in ongoing debates and controversies in the humanities and social sciences.

Already Published

Forthcoming

Why Politics Can't Be Freed From Religion

Ivan Strenski

WILEY-BLACKWELL

A John Wiley & Sons, Ltd., Publication

This edition first published 2010
© 2010 Ivan Strenski

Blackwell Publishing was acquired by John Wiley & Sons in February 2007. Blackwell's publishing program has been merged with Wiley's global Scientific, Technical, and Medical business to form Wiley-Blackwell.

Registered Office
John Wiley & Sons Ltd, The Atrium, Southern Gate, Chichester, West Sussex, PO19 8SQ, United Kingdom

Editorial Offices
350 Main Street, Malden, MA 02148-5020, USA
9600 Garsington Road, Oxford, OX4 2DQ, UK
The Atrium, Southern Gate, Chichester, West Sussex, PO19 8SQ, UK

For details of our global editorial offices, for customer services, and for information about how to apply for permission to reuse the copyright material in this book please see our website at www.wiley.com/wiley-blackwell.

The right of Ivan Strenski to be identified as the author of this work has been asserted in accordance with the UK Copyright, Designs and Patents Act 1988.

All rights reserved. No part of this publication may be reproduced, stored in a retrieval system, or transmitted, in any form or by any means, electronic, mechanical, photocopying, recording or otherwise, except as permitted by the UK Copyright, Designs and Patents Act 1988, without the prior permission of the publisher.

Wiley also publishes its books in a variety of electronic formats. Some content that appears in print may not be available in electronic books.

Designations used by companies to distinguish their products are often claimed as trademarks. All brand names and product names used in this book are trade names, service marks, trademarks or registered trademarks of their respective owners. The publisher is not associated with any product or vendor mentioned in this book. This publication is designed to provide accurate and authoritative information in regard to the subject matter covered. It is sold on the understanding that the publisher is not engaged in rendering professional services. If professional advice or other expert assistance is required, the services of a competent professional should be sought.

Library of Congress Cataloging-in-Publication Data

Strenski, Ivan.
    Why politics can't be freed from religion / Ivan Strenski.
        p.   cm.—(Blackwell manifestos)
    ISBN 978-1-4051-7649-1 (hardcover : alk. paper)—ISBN 978-1-4051-7648-4 (pbk. : alk. paper)
1.   Religion and politics. I.   Title.
    BL65.P7S775 2010
    201′.72—dc22
                                                            2009033874

A catalogue record for this book is available from the British Library.

Set in 11.5/14pt Bembo by SPi Publisher Services, Pondicherry, India
Printed and bound in Malaysia by Vivar Printing Sdn Bhd

01   2010

For my friend, David C. Rapoport

"I don't need a friend who changes when I change
and who nods when I nod;
my shadow does that much better." (Plutarch)

Contents

Contents

Acknowledgments

I would like to acknowledge the support of the following persons and institutions:

Aviel Roshwald, Elisabeth Sifton, Ellen Strenski, Gary Dorrien, George Daughan, Henry Hardy, Holstein Family and Community Endowment, Jon R. Stone, Jonathan L. Walton, Joseph L. Esposito, Lawrence Baron, Linell Cady, Mark Cladis, Mark Juergensmeyer, Maurice Freedman, Nick Allen, Peggy Morgan, Rebecca Harkin, Robert Segal, Senate Faculty Research Lecture Committee of the University of California, Riverside, Steven Engler, Tisa Wenger, Tom Kasulis. In memoriam, Louis Dumont and Ninian Smart.

1

When God Plays Politics
Radical Interrogations
of Religion, Power, and Politics

I am writing these words from Los Angeles, a city boasting the largest ex-patriot Iranian population in the world. It is late June, 2009. Half a world away, but close in mind, are the mass demonstrations against the contested presidential election 'won' by President Ahmadinejad. By Twitter, Facebook, cell phone, video-cam or cable news, we all learn about, and even directly see, events unfolding on the streets of Tehran, Tabriz, and Isfahan, events whose outcome is unclear. Yet, what is clear to all is another struggle between the brute force of police and militias versus the massed moral forces unleashed by a feeling of being wronged. 'Power' is speaking in its own language to 'truth.'

As someone with a lifelong interest in the puzzles of human knowledge, I have always tried to ask myself what it is I *'see'* when I *'look'* at something. What do I understand, how do I make sense or give an account of what passes before my eyes? Likewise, as a person with an equally long interest in both religion and politics, I make even greater demands on myself to get at what I *'see'* when I *'look'* at these images from faraway Iran. How do I *understand* what the events in Iran, June 2009, present to my eyes? Do I just 'see' politics? And, if so, what is it to 'see' something 'political' when I 'look' at the demonstrations, the padlocked ballot boxes, the placards in English: "I want my vote," the leaders claiming election and others admitting defeat, or when I hear of demonstrators calling out "death to the dictator"? Can I 'see' only 'politics' in images of

1

turbaned Shi'i mullahs, venerable ayatollahs, 'covered' women, and hear talk of 'martyrs' and 'sacrifice' or learn of the night-time calls of "Allah-u-akbar!" ringing from rooftops all over the city? Can all this that I 'look' upon really be 'seen' or best understood from one and only one angle – as 'politics'? Clearly not.

As the days pass, the theocracy in power seeks to impose its will, but, in doing so, is creating its own religious mirror-image – the powerless, yet mighty, martyrs among the fallen. For every demonstrator killed, another martyr is born. For every demonstrator that 'power' feels it has removed from the struggle, another martyr is mourned and another 'spiritual' being comes to life. In the face of the *potestas* of the *Basiji* thug-militia, wielding truncheons against scattered packs of the defenseless, come cries of resistance to lying, fraud, and domination, speaking in the idiom of ultimate authority: *'Allah-u-akbar!'*

If this politics of Tehran June 2009 is *just* 'politics,' it is an unusual sort of politics – one with few parallels in today's Western world. Maybe the demonstrations of the 1980s in the shipyards of Gdansk come close? There, Solidarity strikers chanted slogans of defiance against a regime, while hoisting aloft images of John Paul II or the Blessed Virgin of Częstohowa in the faces of governmental para-militaries. Images of the black civil rights demonstrations of the 1960s, led as they were by clergy singing hymns usually reserved for the chapel, likewise flash before our memory.

Such a 'politics,' equally well 'seen' as 'religious,' raises questions. Are there in fact such wholly different things as religion and politics? Is our distinction between the two really any more sustainable, say, than that between 'religion' and 'cult'? Like efforts to separate 'religion' from 'cult,' might not our distinction between 'religion' and 'politics' be only a device for manipulating one or the other? 'Politics,' it is said, has no place in a 'religious' house of worship; 'religion,' likewise, belongs to the private and personal sphere, not to the public square in which we do 'politics.' But, then we are hit with news from Iran. State 'politicians' invoke the sacral authority vested in them as clerics; demonstrators chanting 'Allah-u-akbar!'

protest the results of an election for president of a republic. Is one 'religious' and the other 'political'? And, if so, which is which? Maybe, our distinctions between religion and politics just do not work for Iran? Maybe, recalling Solidarity or Dr. King, they don't even work for us? Or, do they?

And, moreover, if we do decide to classify events as 'political' or 'religious,' what are we admitting about our larger view of the world in doing so? Most often it seems that we imagine that religion and politics are objectively two distinct things, like two 'tools' – a hammer and a nail. So, some have said that if both religion and politics are at play in Tehran, Gdansk, or Selma, for example, religion is being *'used'* for political purposes, *'used'* by political forces to 'hammer' their opponents. A blogger, writing on a website devoted to keeping watch on Michigan Congressman Thaddeus McCotter, complains in this way: "Politics is an ugly business. Religion is a beautiful one. So when a politician audaciously attempts to use religion to advance his political agenda, citizens should be outraged." (Blogger 2008) The Reverend Pat Robertson has gone to the extreme of arguing that Islam is so thoroughly 'used' these days for 'political' purposes that it has lost its 'religious' self and become totally political. "We have to recognize that Islam is not," Robertson says, "a religion. It is a worldwide political movement meant on domination of the world." (Robertson 2007) The political 'hammer' of Islam has driven the religious 'nail' right out of sight.

Conversely, others have complained that religion has *used* politics, that something essentially otherworldly has become something contrary to its nature – politicized. The common charge against the Christian Right has been that they have tried to grasp the hammer of 'political' power to pound out their own religious purposes. Take over the local board of education and forbid the teaching of Darwinian evolution in the public schools; gain a majority in the statehouse and outlaw abortion, same sex marriage, and the like. Not long ago, the election of John F. Kennedy, as the first Roman Catholic president, was feared to be a plot to usher in a papal takeover of the nation. Suspicions of the political intentions of the Vatican are sometimes as strong as they are of the Christian Right. A blog comment from a reader, Robert Singer, responding to Michele Madigan Somerville's "Born Again in Brooklyn" in the *New York Times* reminds us of this fear. Singer bluntly characterizes the Roman Catholic Church as a "political church ... ruled by political bishops, cardinals and pope." (Letter from Robert Singer 2009) Religious hammer, political nail.

So, as we "look" at the Tehran demonstrations, what do we really 'see'? Do we 'see' such political manipulation or *use* of 'religion' by either side? Do we 'see' an essentially "ugly" politics of the regime when we 'look' at paramilitaries confronting people espousing a basically "beautiful" religion of peaceful demonstration? Or, do we 'see' the "ugly" politicized religion of the mullahs exposed as no authentic religion at all, but merely something used to mask the politics of domination played by the regime? Further, do we perhaps 'see' the religion of the demonstrators as "beautiful" precisely because, unlike politics, it is something intimate and deeply believed, not some disguise for an underlying 'politics' of Western secularism? Or, do we 'see' religion on the streets of Tehran as "beautiful" precisely because, like the marches led by Dr. Martin Luther King, Jr. or Gandhi, it engaged life bravely in the salvation of the public world? The questions do not stop in Tehran. Given a similar kind of mass movement, what did we 'see' when we 'looked' on in Tiananmen Square, June 1989? On the part of the demonstrators, was this just 'politics' too? Was it 'politics' devoid of 'religion,' and thus unlike the odd 'politics' of Gdansk, Tehran, and Selma? When 'Tank Man,' that lone figure, dodging before an advancing tank, threatened to bring it to a halt by the authority invested in him as a human being, were we 'seeing' what we 'saw' in Gdansk, Tehran, or the American South? Some would say that Tank Man's practical declaration of the sacredness of his individual humanity counts as 'religious' as much as an image of the Blessed Virgin or a cry of "Allah-u-akbar!".

These questions cannot, however, be answered straightaway. The reason they cannot be answered as they stand has nothing to do

with the *facts* from which the questions proceed. We would not be closer to answers if we knew more about Tank Man, Dr. King, Gandhi, or the demonstrators in Tehran. The reason these questions cannot be answered is because our concepts of religion and politics (and power) are systematically conflicted or unclear, and our uses of these terms are burdened with unexamined assumptions. To begin addressing the questions that come at us about religion and politics, we need, first, to do a good deal of preliminary sorting out of how we think about religion, power, and politics. We need to query our assumptions, for example, about our way of talking about 'power' as a unified field; we need to query the common clichés that surround 'religion' – that it is something essentially good (or bad), a reality internal, private, and reducible to having certain beliefs; we need to challenge the presumption that politics is autonomous and superior to other dimensions of life, such as morality, economics, or religion; we need as well to ask why we should go along with the common-place view that 'everything is political.' Such is this book's purpose.

This book is not, then, about the *particularities* of 'religion' in this or that place or time. Not only am I unprepared to write a book on religion and politics, say, in the 'I-countries' – Ireland, Israel, India, Indonesia, Iran, Iraq, Ingushetia, and so on – but such books have been done aplenty. 'Been there and done that.' So, how would another *kind* of book on religion and politics look? To make a difference, such a book would have to treat religion and politics *generally*. But, in being *general* how could it avoid the fatuous, sweeping generalizations of books that pontificate from their privileged God's eye view of our world? It would be downright foolhardy to attempt a book that pretended to encompass religion and politics globally – before even thinking critically about how we use the words 'religion' and 'politics,' and examining the assumptions that lie buried under the surface of our everyday talk of religion and politics. So, what I do in this book is to think critically about the basic categories of religion, power, and politics.

I shall also try to go further. The participants in all these events in Tehran, Selma, Gdansk, and Tiananmen Square were all, in their own ways, playing 'politics,' and there may be compelling reasons to draw some distinctions between these 'ways.' On the one side, the irresistible force of sheer coercive power; on the other, the immovable object of headstrong (and 'heart-strong') resistance of spirit. But, are these kinds of agency different enough to merit different names, or are they plays of 'power' in the same register? Are they even perhaps different 'things' or only two kinds of the same 'thing'? Is it so absurd to say that on the one side, *politics* is arrayed in its most fearsome and characteristic attire – sheer power, coercive force, *potestas*? On the other, do we not recognize in moral commitment and vision 'weapons of the spirit,' *religious* conviction, a stubborn insistence upon legitimacy, the willingness to recognize worthy (*auctoritas*) authority, the belief that some things are to be treasured as sacred? This book takes its rise from the perception of such distinctions in the array of agency in our world. Without laying down hard and fast, abstract, definitions and distinctions of religion and politics, I shall seek to grasp what we might possibly mean in distinguishing them from each other, or alternately in declaring the two part of the same thing. What does it *add* to the way we 'see' the events in Tehran, June 2009, to label them 'religious' as well as 'political'? What are we trying to bring out when we say that we 'see' something 'religious' amid the 'political'?

I shall accordingly try to contribute to a discussion of the kinds of questions I have raised by delving into the basic notions of religion, power, and politics so that we can unpack – and sort out – the baggage of meanings with which they are laden. But having unpacked these notions, this book is about sorting through them for the sake of better thinking about religion and politics. This entire process of sifting through our categories is what I call 'interrogation.' Accordingly, in the next chapter, I shall 'interrogate' the concept of 'religion' both as it has been current in everyday language and as it has been lately regarded in the academic world. In Chapter 3, 'power' will be similarly interrogated, as will 'politics' in Chapter 4. Once thus interrogated, however, I do not let matters stand. Concepts are things to be used to grapple with the world, and not just abstract objects of critical contemplation. Word play may be fine at a party, but it is useless in a struggle. I am writing this book in part because I feel that there are many struggles to which we privileged intellectuals have a responsibility to respond. While it is vital, therefore, to think *about* our categories – to 'interrogate' religion, power, and politics – I want us to think *with* them as well. It is in thinking *with* critical notions in our world, and in adding our thoughts to the universe of discourse of both the university and the community at large, that we as intellectuals take a responsible part in public discourse. In the final chapter, I shall, therefore, try to show how the 'thinking *about*' religion, power, and politics of Chapters 2, 3, and 4, respectively, can enrich the 'thinking with' religion, power, and politics of Chapter 5 in the test case of suicide bombers in the Middle East.

2

Interrogating 'Religion'

People do not really fight about religion. If they seem to be doing so, they must really be fighting about something else. (Bossy 1991, 267–85, 278)

Newspeak was the official language of Oceania, and had been devised to meet the ideological needs of Ingsoc, or English Socialism … As we have already seen in the case of the word free, words which had once borne a heretical meaning were sometimes retained for the sake of convenience, but only with the undesirable meanings purged out of them. Countless other words such as honour, justice, morality, internationalism, democracy, science, and religion had simply ceased to exist. (Orwell 1948, 267–79)

1. Religion Trouble

Commonsense tells us that we know very well – thank you very much! – what religion is. Just open up the Yellow Pages of any phone directory and *'look'* under 'religion.' Or, try Googling. There, over 367 million 'religion' entries are ready to satisfy one's curiosity. Narrowing the search to the "definition of religion" cuts the 367 million down by a factor of 50 or so, but still turns up 7 million items. Or, if we want to stick to academic sources, why not just 'look' to the indices and tables of contents of most books from the social and behavioral sciences and report what comes up as 'religion' there as well? As good empiricists, many doing 'social research' survey work resist imposing categories, but instead test those readily understandable in everyday speech. If asked what 'religion' they are, researchers assume respondents know the definition of the word.

Here are cases, however, where commonsense and everyday speech can lead us badly astray. We can always take a word like 'religion,' so to speak, 'off the shelf' of everyday speech or out of the ether of the internet. But, what do we *'see'* when we do so? What does this tell us about *why* a certain item finds its way to the Yellow Pages, or *why* an item finds itself amidst the riotous throng of 367 million 'religion' entries in Google? What *rules* does Google's Great Decider follow to determine what gets added to that endless list of entries under 'religion'? And, even if we could delve into the Google Mind to learn how it decided to include something as 'religion' in its search, how would we know that the Google Mind was right in doing so? Thus, the commonplaces of everyday speech or the search results of a Google may be reasonable places to *begin* to define or pick out what 'religion' might be, but they can never satisfy the most basic question about definition – *why* something is or is not to be counted as 'religion.' Search engines have a limited role. They leave us blind about what we really *'see,'* when we *'look'* at what they yield.

Defining 'religion' then perhaps may be something better left to professionals, to learned people, such as those behind *The HarperCollins Dictionary of Religion*? Surely, such a massive volume should improve upon commonsense or everyday understanding of what 'religion' is? Surely, it should be able to tell us what we *'see'* when we *'look'* at 'religion'? The results, as I shall show, are not particularly impressive. Although promising to do better than settling for everyday commonsense uses of 'religion,' the *Dictionary*'s approach to the definition of religion exposes the weaknesses of most attempts to go beyond commonsense. In the entry "religion, definition of," the *Dictionary* begins by rightly observing that definitions of religion often mistakenly aim to be capacious and inclusive. But, sadly, in doing so, religion is seen as "just about anything.""Religion' is ""ultimate concern' or 'worldview'," or seen as expressing an ""oceanic feeling,' or 'the feeling of absolute dependence."" In short, a very broad definition of religion yields an ambiguous notion without discernable boundaries. (Anon. 1995, 893–4) When, on the other hand, others try to restrict the definition, the *Dictionary* scores the results for being "too restrictive or limited." Defining 'religion' as 'belief in God' might succeed in avoiding being vague, but fails because it is too narrow – say because it left out Theravāda Buddhism, a supposedly non-theistic religion. (Anon. 1995, 893–4, 893)

Yet, even when the *Dictionary* attempts to define 'religion' for itself by being neither too broad nor too narrow, it hardly fares better. It proposes to define 'religion' as a "system of beliefs and practices that are relative to superhuman beings."This, the *Dictionary* thinks includes Theravāda Buddhism, because some scholars believe that in practice, if not in theory, Theravāda Buddhism does reserve a special place for 'superhuman beings.' (Anon. 1995, 893–4, 894) The *Dictionary* is, however, suspiciously silent about certain worldviews and modern ideologies, such as fascism, Maoism, nationalism, or ancient non-theistic systems, such as Jainism, Sāmkhya, Zen, Daoism, and normative Theravāda Buddhism. Why are not these 'religions' too, as Ninian Smart has argued? (Smart 1983) The persistence of both ambiguous and narrow ways of thinking about religion, then, presents us with a stiff challenge. Were that not enough challenge, what do we do in a book, like the present one, which endeavors to advance understanding of situations in which both religion and politics seem to be at play?

I shall argue, along with the *Dictionary*, that commonsense ideas about the nature of religion are indeed, on the one hand, too vague, confusing, or numerous to be useful and, on the other, often so narrow as to be more or less wrong. But, how do we do better than even the *Dictionary* itself has done? While I do not believe that *precise definition* of our concepts is critical to fruitful thinking, I do believe that we can be *accurate* enough in our thinking to engage

10

religion and politics fruitfully. But reaching a level of sufficient *accuracy* will mean that we will need to make trouble for our concepts. I think, for example, that we need to go about defining how we use the word 'religion' by considering the larger context of the strategies of our thinking. I am urging us to abandon the view that 'religion' is some thing that can or ought to be defined in the abstract. Instead, 'religion' is a term that needs to be defined variously as contexts and strategies of inquiry change.

But unlike most critics of the concept of 'religion,' I shall also argue that terms like 'power' and 'politics,' typically meant to replace 'religion,' are in a similarly woeful state. Ironically, it will be in historicizing them that they will show their roots in religion. This conceptual disarray, nevertheless, leaves anyone wishing to talk coherently about religion and politics in a considerable quandary. How do we engage issues of religion and politics if we cannot define these terms? By troubling our notions of religion, power, and politics, I think I can show how we can think and say consequential things about religion and politics – mostly because we will have attended to the larger purposes of our thinking. This chapter is then devoted both to how to trouble received notions of 'religion' and to how to retrieve some notion of 'religion' useful for engaging 'politics.'

2. 'Seeing' Religion: Six Common Clichés

The first item on the agenda is a thorough 'house cleaning' of the way conventional wisdom *'sees'* religion when it *'looks'* at the world. This is a 'house cleaning' that, in effect, sweeps out ways of defining religion, and then seeks to install new ones. Such everyday ways of *'seeing'* religion are, as we will see, false, misleading, inadequate, hackneyed, uninformed, and more. Yet, because of their long history of use in the West, these ways of *'seeing'* religion and thus defining it are hard to clear out of our discourse about religion. These otherwise normal and commonsense ways of *'seeing'* religion have

11

staying power. They have been shaped by specific theoretical and theological interests in the West, with all the institutional support such activities can muster from both state and ecclesiastical social formations. Thus established, I have settled upon what I think are the six most common ways that conventional wisdom defines or *'sees'* religion. I refer to them as six *clichés* that define the way we should *'see'* religion. Here's my list.

A set of two assumptions make up the first and second clichés; they mirror themselves as flip-sides of each other. First cliché: religion is necessarily and by definition good; second cliché: religion is, on the contrary, always bad. On the basis of the first assumption people will tend to *excuse* religion from blame for almost anything deemed bad – war, racism, intolerance, anti-Semitism, terrorism, and such. Familiar to our ears is constant talk of how 'religion' is good, but on occasion has been 'hijacked' or 'used' by political extremists for their evil-doing. The slogans that all religions are 'religions of peace' and that religion is merely 'used' by evil politicians are other variants on this assumption. Those holding the second assumption merely invert the first: religion is to be blamed for everything, or virtually everything, that goes wrong.

The third and fourth unexamined assumptions form a pair as well, but these complement, rather than oppose one another. Here, most people suppose that religion is, thirdly, mainly a matter of beliefs (and relatedly, feelings or 'experiences'), rather than rituals or religious practices. Jonathan Z. Smith has argued that, in the West, we might mark a shift from a Catholic, mostly Spanish, practice of conceiving religion as "careful performance of ritual obligations," to a Protestant conception of religion as "belief." (Smith 2004, 179–96, 181ff.) Thus, religion is to be characterized in creed-like statements or reports about feelings or other inner states of mind and heart. Talal Asad has, for instance, characterized Protestant Christians as feeling that belief is "a purely inner, private state of mind, a particular state of mind detached from everyday practices." (Asad 1996, 1–15, 10ff.)

Complementing this definition of religion as belief is the idea that those beliefs, feelings, and experiences constituting religion are, fourthly, anchored by the central belief in God. Thus, whenever I ask my students for a definition of religion, the vast majority are guaranteed to reply, to no one's surprise, "the belief in God." If confronted with 'religions' where rituals, practices, special kinds of social unit, or other forms of embodiment such as works of art and architecture are prominent, these representatives of 'religion' of this kind were ready with all manner of assault. On this well-worn view, such things as rituals, practices, and such are mere 'externals,' and at best only come to life and have any meaning because of the beliefs, feelings, and experiences informing and animating them. As such, any expression of such 'externals' amounted to what Liberal Protestant thinkers called a "religious materialism." And as such, liberal Christianity set a prevailing tone of suspicion that a religion grounded in ritual observance and practices, for example, is "always more or less superstitious." (Réville 1874, 138–56, 151) For these Liberal Protestant theologians, a really religious person would inform their sensibility with a religious "spiritualism" which, to them, results from a "more elevated moral and religious sense." (Réville 1874, 138–56, 154)

The fifth and six unexamined assumptions follow naturally from those already mooted. Given that belief, feelings, and experience characterize religion, and given that these are private, 'internal' matters, religion is, fifth, considered private or 'deeply personal' as well. Nineteenth-century Protestant theologians proudly proclaimed the absolute insulation of religion from the external world of power and conflict. From "the inmost depths of our souls," said one of Liberal Protestantism's leading representatives, religion radiates a "power ... which the assaults of the keenest of the adversaries of religion with the keenest shafts of their wit, with all their learning and eloquence ... are in the long-run unavailing and impotent." (Tiele 1898, 24) Religion therefore dwelt in the secret redoubt of "the heart" – an impregnable and autonomous fortress

13

fashioned by the liberal Protestant piety of the day, thus rendering it ultimately resistant to inquiry. (Tiele 1898, 14)

As such, in its essence, religion is, sixth and finally, separate from power and politics, since they are typically public, embodied, and external. Talal Asad goes so far as to claim that the "separation of religion from power is a modern Western norm." (Asad 1993, 28) Religion is a matter of something called 'spirit'; it is the very essence of the 'spiritual' dimension of life, after all. As a result, religion is not naturally something that trucks with power. 'Power' belongs to the realm of the profane.

Whatever one's feelings about them, these common suppositions about religion deserve scrutiny, not least of all because they each figure substantially in how people conceive questions about religion and politics. Any effort to approach questions of religion and politics will have to contend with them. And, any effort, moreover, to do what I have called 'interrogate' concepts like religion, politics, or power will also have to take stock of such ordinary unexamined assumptions in the minds of people. Let me then begin my 'interrogation' projects by interrogating 'religion' – by taking on these six clichés about religion in this chapter.

3. Gagging at the Feast of Two Unexamined Assumptions: Religion, All Good or All Bad

a. The religion-is-good cliché

Although many liberals and conservatives often bitterly disagree over a whole range of issues concerning religion in politics, many make unexpected common cause in being 'politically correct' about at least one part of the relationship of religion to politics. They both agree that religion is necessarily good, and ought never to be criticized or confronted on occasions where religion and politics bond together. As we will see, this cliché lies at the basis of a number of other myths about religion and politics. A prominent variant of the religion-is-good thesis is that all religions are so-called 'religions of peace.' This holds that religions are essentially peaceful, while only political entities are violent or war-loving. Prime evidence of a religion's corruption by politics and institutionalization would be its politicization – everything from Constantine's 'Churchianity' to the Christian Right and Jihadi Islam. As President George W. Bush said before a joint session of the Congress on 20 September 2001:

> I also want to speak tonight directly to Muslims throughout the world. We respect your faith. It's practiced freely by many millions of Americans, and by millions more in countries that America counts as friends. Its teachings are good and peaceful, and those who commit evil in the name of Allah blaspheme the name of Allah. (Applause.) (Bush 2001 Speech)

Of course, a few moments' historical reflection will poke massive holes in the assumption that religion is necessarily peaceful, and that politics is always warlike. This cliché reflects ignorance of the history of Christianity in the Middle Ages, where, as historian John Neville Figgis could say, the "real State of the Middle Ages in the modern sense – if the words are not a paradox – is the Church." (Figgis 1998, 15) As the 'real' temporal 'power' for hundreds of years of Christian history, the Church fielded its armies and Crusaders, fought its wars against fellow Christians and non-Christians alike; in short, did all those things that show what a warring religion could be. As we will see in the next chapter, the papal "claim to an inherent right to political power" was longstanding in the history of the West. It entailed nothing short of a change "in the relation of the divine to the earthly: the divine now claims to rule the world through the Church." The Church takes its place among the worldly powers of the day. (Dumont 1986a, 23–59, 50) Figgis even goes so far as to claim that the divine right of kings was, in this way, first claimed by the pope. (Figgis 1998, 29) Thus, if Figgis is correct, in the Carolingian West we get the "kingly priesthood" of the Roman Church, or the "papal monarchy" of Colin Morris's description, and thus a religious body fully able to be as 'bad' as any 'political' body one might name. (Dumont 1986a, 23–59, 50; Morris 1989, 1)

Witness alone the confidence of Pope Urban addressing the congregation of Vallombrosa, October 7, 1096 in the First Crusade. First, informing the "knights" of their duties to fight for Christianity, Pope Urban says,

> We have heard that some of you want to set out with the knights who are making for Jerusalem with the intention of liberating Christianity. This is the right kind of sacrifice, but it is planned by the wrong kind of person. For we were stimulating the minds of knights to go on this expedition, since they might be able to restrain the savagery of the Saracens by their arms and restore the Christians to their former freedom.

But, equally well, Pope Urban informs the clergy of his displeasure at the plans of some to participate as well in the holy war. But, Urban continues,

> we do not want those who have abandoned the world and have vowed themselves to spiritual warfare either to bear arms or to go on this journey; we go so far as to forbid them to do so. And we forbid religious – clerics or monks – to set out in this company without the permission of their bishops or abbots in accordance with the rule of the holy canons. (Urban II 1981, 37–40, cited in Riley-Smith & Riley-Smith 1981, 37)

Both these directives are fully acts of a religious kind, delivered by the most conspicuously religious figure in Christianity – the pope himself. We, in our own time, may not *like* this kind of warring religion – we might not think this is *'belief'* – but we must simply face the fact that Christianity has a long history in being just such a religion.

At the very least, the belief in religion as necessarily belief reflects a theological strategy derived from precisely the kind of Christianity which sought to define the faith against the medieval model of a fully political entity ruling by divine right. In particular, the belief in religion's goodness reflects this parochial cultural conviction typical of the West, stemming at least from the Reformation and reinforced heavily by nineteenth-century liberal Protestantism. As such, it fails the 'Says who?' test. In addition to medieval Christianity, religions such as Judaism or Islam do not traditionally dichotomize themselves and other religions in the same way. Their religious leaders, their 'prophets' – Moses, Muhammad – are often 'armed,' unlike the Jesus who turns the other cheek (but not the Jesus of the Book of Revelation or the warrior saints of the Catholic Middle Ages) or the Buddha who withdraws from active engagement in violence. Such images of religious violence lead to questioning the assumption that all religions are religions of peace. Why should we not embrace another paradigm of religion – as also worldly, political, and violent, and assume the priority of 'armed prophecy' rather than those that seem to dominate our current discourse by privileging religion as defined by an interiorizing spirituality? In addition to the Crusades, think only of the abolitionist, John Brown, the Jewish fighters of the Warsaw Ghetto, the belligerents of the Nichiren Shōshū Sōka Gakkai, the Ghost Dancers, Muhammad and his Companions, the Zealots, the Jesus who promised "not peace, but a sword."

What is more, there is something deeply ironic about the historical course taken by so-called religions of peace. Even in cases where a hard distinction between the internal and external might be made, and where we can speak of a peaceful, spiritualist, even quietist, religion, these 'peaceful' religions sometime seem more like a politics waiting to happen, a politics with the 'engine idling,' so to speak. Consider Martin Luther King, Jr.'s American civil rights movement as a thoroughly and simultaneously religious and political phenomenon, even if 'unarmed.' Where, then, is the internal, where the external? Has such language far outlived any usefulness it might have had? When a Protestant minister, a Jewish rabbi, and a Catholic priest lead a march against segregation in the American south, or when Archbishop Desmond Tutu does the equivalent in apartheid South Africa, do the categories of 'internal' and 'external' make any sense? Of course, before Martin Luther King, Jr.'s movement took active shape in the 1960s, we might have referred to the apolitical or quietist character of the Black churches as 'internal,' since they shied away from the political action that would characterize them in their marching and demonstrating days. But even in that withdrawn form, might we not see the religion of the Black church, inspired and informed as it was by the vigorous biblical imagery of ancient Israel's struggle for liberation and the Hebrew Bible's prophets demanding justice, as a politics in embryo, as a politics with only the 'engine idling,' as a politics 'a rarin' to go' – however non-violent its politics turned out to be?

b. Politics "using" religion: Anatomy of a cliché

Contained in the cliché that religion is 'good' is the complaint that, however good religion may be, it is often 'used' or 'manipulated' by unscrupulous politicians. Recently, for example, a controversy erupted over cartoons of Muhammad published in a Danish newspaper. The artist's motive for drawing them appealed explicitly to this notion of religion being "used" by politics. Thus, the cartoonist, Kurt Westergaard, said in the *New York Times* that "'With this drawing, I wanted to show how fanatical Islamists or terrorists use religion as a kind of spiritual weapon.'" (Anon. 2008, A11) Similarly, in the wake of 9/11, prominent liberals joined President Bush in deflecting blame for the bombings from Islam, partly in a laudable spirit of religious tolerance, but also, it seems, because, to both, religion can do no wrong. Religion is necessarily belief, and any religion that seems to be 'bad' must not be 'true' or 'real' religion. Thus, on 9/11, religion – here Islam – had been used again, but this time 'hijacked.' It had been diverted from its 'true' nature and corrupted in some 'evil' way. Continuing in his address before the Congress on September 20, 2001, President Bush said, "The terrorists are traitors to their own faith, trying, in effect, to hijack Islam itself. The enemy of America is not our many Muslim friends; it is not our many Arab friends. Our enemy is a radical network of terrorists, and every government that supports them. (Applause.)" (Bush 2001 Speech) Thus, the attacks of the Muslim 'human bombers' of 9/11, despite their chanting Quranic verses and keening ritually as they plunged toward the twin towers in lower Manhattan, somehow did not represent any sort of 'real' face of Islam, the fulfillment of any real purposes of an Islamic sort. Similarly, the Crusades or the Ku Klux Klan do not in any way represent 'real' interests or purposes of Christianity. Absurdly, on this view, the hijackers of 9/11 were not 'real' Muslims either, because the murderous tactics and deeds they performed were 'bad.' Nor were the Crusaders 'real' Christians, since they did not pursue certain Christian moral goals, or a strategy of spreading loving kindness and charity. But who were the 9/11 hijackers but self-styled soldiers of Islam, embarked on a strategy of waging *jihad?* Were they, perhaps, only Arabs, instead, and nothing more? Were they perhaps only testosterone-charged young males, and nothing more? And, who, as well, were the Crusaders but Christian soldiers, 'marching as to war'? Were they perhaps only Franks, and nothing more – only soldiers of fortune, and nothing more? One of the ways that religions try to protect themselves from challenges to their innate belief in goodness, purity, and virtue is by wheeling in defensive ways of disclaiming responsibility for otherwise characterized political actions, even though in its intrinsic nature religion is felt to be good, while politics is blamed for the problems.

In the same vein, despite their recent engagement in politics in the United States, American Evangelical Christians have warned their own members of the dangers of being "used" for political purposes:

> The other error, made by both the religious left and the religious right in recent decades, is to politicize faith, using faith to express essentially political points that have lost touch with biblical truth. That way faith loses its independence, the church becomes "the regime at prayer," Christians become "useful idiots" for one political party or another, and the Christian faith becomes an ideology in its purest form. Christian beliefs are used as weapons for political interests. (Evangelical & Committee 2008, 1–20, 15)

I believe that when we look more closely at such claims, we find them to be incoherent. Most claims that religion has been 'used,' therefore, boil down to the reality of religious people simply *not liking* the particular arrangements they have made – for the most part, willingly – with political entities. What had once been an eagerly devoured 'sweet deal' now leaves a 'sour taste' in the mouth.

The implications of this viewpoint, however, intended as it may be to protect and preserve the reputation of religion, serves only to diminish it. Therefore, when those committed to the religion-is-good thesis see cases in which religion does not look good, they conclude that it is being misrepresented by being "used" by politics or politicians. Religion and politics are seen as alien to one another. Religion has been the victim of exploitation and made to behave contrary to its 'true' nature. On this view, religion is thus cast as something passive. It is a mere 'tool,' like a hammer, that one can take up or throw down. Like a hammer, religion is an inert object of 'utility,' serving the agent purposes of other forces or persons. And, like a hammer, again, with respect to the carpenter wielding it, religion has no intrinsic connection to the human political agent 'wielding' it. Such language makes sense when one speaks of institutions dominating each other, such as the concrete apparatuses of 'church' and 'state'. In today's Iran, commentators speak of a struggle between "the republican essence of Iran and its clerical oligarchy." (Jahanbegloo 2009, A25) In Luther's time, we can also speak of the struggle between ecclesiastical institutions and state institutions, such as a particular dynastic house.

But, unfortunately, those who use 'religion' in the abstract sense often get it wrong. They claim to see 'religion' as something merely "used" by politics, but they do not see that short of speaking of specific concrete institutions, it is hard to know what such assertions mean. They cannot imagine, for example, religious motives being organically woven into a complex process or strategy, involving all sorts of other aspects of human life, like the arts, politics, economics, and such. Was the religious aspect of Mussolini's fascism just a 'tool' wielded for political purposes? Or was religion rather, as Emilio Gentile has exhaustively argued, woven integrally into the whole of Mussolini's purposes – ones that melded art, oratory, ritual, architecture, music, military force, and such into 'fascism'?

(Gentile 1996) Beyond the conceptual and empirical incoherence of the "religion-as-used" thesis, which I now will expose, I should think that most religious people would be straightaway repelled by the implications of this point of view. Were the "religion-as-used" thesis true – which I do not believe – religion would be such a feeble thing in the minds of religious folk that one would seriously wonder why anyone would honor it!

4. The Religion-Is-No-Good Cliché

Equally disabling – but opposite – to the religion-is-good cliché is the latest cliché foisted upon us – that religion-is-no-good. Lately, in a flurry of works by the emotionally evangelical "new atheists," such as Richard Dawkins, Daniel Dennett, Sam Harris, and Christopher Hitchens, the reading public has been treated to a wholesale broadside campaign of denunciations of religion worthy of being organized under the rubric as the 'religion-is-no-good' school. (Dawkins 2006; Dennett 2007; Harris 2006; Hitchens 2007) Since it is Hitchens who takes on 'religion' most often for its failings in the social and political world, a few examples from his naughtily entitled work, *God Is Not Great,* might give one an idea of what strategy the religion-is-no-good writers pursue. Consider this tidy summation of Hitchens' complaints for starters:

> There … remain four irreducible objections to religious faith: that it wholly misrepresents the origins of man and the cosmos, that because of this original error it manages to combine the maximum of servility with the maximum of solipsism, that it is both the cause of dangerous sexual repression, and that it is ultimately grounded on wish-thinking. (Hitchens 2007, 4)

Another choice 'slam' clobbers religion on its ethical side:

> We believe with certainty that an ethical life can be lived without religion. And we know for a fact that the corollary holds true – that

21

religion has caused innumerable people not just to conduct themselves no better than others, but to award themselves permission to behave in ways that would make a brothel-keeper or an ethnic cleanser raise an eyebrow. (Hitchens 2007, 6)

My last example gives voice to where Hitchens stands on the proposition that religion-is-bad. It is "poison":

As I write these words, and as you read them, people of faith are in their different ways planning your and my destruction, and the destruction of all the hard-won human attainments that I have touched upon. *Religion poisons everything.* (Hitchens 2007, 13)

With words like these, it is hard to see how Hitchens could see religion as any good for anything – how religion of any description could fulfill any good purposes. "Religion is red in both tooth and claw" is an insinuation that has about as much admiration for it and its role in history as Hitchens was willing to grant it.

The easiest way to get reasonable purchase on these charges is to select one and expose the shallow opportunism of the "new atheists" into the bargain. Hitchens, for instance, says that religion "wholly misrepresents the origins of man and the cosmos." Just what religion Hitchens has in mind, he does not say, because as his broadside attack implies, he defines 'religions' as if they were the same. But, first, is Hitchens right to assume the definition of 'religion' presumed in his charge? Hitchens is way off base. Theravāda Buddhism, for instance, utterly disdains any speculation about human and cosmic origins. For the Buddhists, the cosmos and all that it contains are a kind of mystery in which they have no interest at all, since they are irrelevant to the central existential problems of human life.

Hitchens might well complain – unfairly as it happens – that I have selected an exceptional 'boundary' case by embracing Theravāda Buddhism within my definition of 'religion.' What about those religions, such as Christianity, that conform to Hitchens' definition? Do they not think they know how the world and all that's in it came about? Here, we must refuse the assumption that Christians, for example, are committed to some sort of quasi-scientific, matter-of-fact account of human and cosmic origins – to a *belief* about such things. Despite the various creedal declarations of "believing in God, Creator of heaven and earth," nowhere does scripture itself say how those words are to be interpreted, any more than it says how the Genesis account of creation in seven days is to be read. Are these statements to be read like legal documents, such as deeds, or perhaps like good fantasy stories or science fiction? Hitchens just assumes the former. Why could it not be the latter? Who said that Genesis had to be read like history or, indeed, a biology textbook?! And, if it be the former, how precisely does he know – rather than simply believing it himself – that Genesis is not closer to the mark than what he believes? 'Big Bang,' anyone? One wonders what Hitchens might have said in the heat of the first proposals of Big Bang theory. Perhaps a little humility might be in order – especially given the fact that the Big Bang theory was in part motivated by the creationist perspective of one of its chief proposers, the Belgian priest Father Georges-Henri Lemaître, in 1894.

When it comes to social and political matters, Hitchens fares no better. When he claims that "people of faith are in their different ways planning your and my destruction," he does not simply have the human bombers of 9/11 in mind. Are the Quakers sharpening their long knives? Are the Zen Buddhists readying some 'explod-ing' koan meant to blow our minds? Perhaps the Amish are groom-ing their horses for some sort of cavalry charge against the local Apple store? What gives Hitchens the gall to say that *"Religion poisons everything"* (Hitchens 2007, 13)? Clearly, Hitchens nurses some sort of strategy of 'destruction' of his own. To balance Hitchens' rage against Christianity, let me also refer readers again to the work of historians who have uncovered the roots of cardinal ideals of the liberal secular state that grew organically out of the history of Christianity in the West. One showed how the belief in the fundamental "equality of" all peoples, that people have rights equal to that of the emperor and so on, grew historically out of Roman

Catholic Natural Law. Similarly, the general rule of law, the contractual theory of legitimacy, an international law itself — to which both pope and emperor were subject, arises from the same source (Figgis 1998, 7) The religion-is-no-good rant of the "new atheists" does not stand up any better than the special pleading of the religion-is-good crowd. A curse on both their houses.

5. The Second Set of Two Clichés: Religion Is Belief and Belief in God

a. Beliefs, creeds and the modern 'essence' of religion

Ever since the dawn of the modern era in the West, and considerably earlier by some reckonings, religion has been understood essentially to be constituted by beliefs, creeds, doctrines, dogmas, confessional statements, and the like. Historian of Christianity Jaroslav Pelikan has recently published a 600-page volume collecting the hundreds of such documents qualifying as statements of *belief* in the Christian tradition alone. (Pelikan 2003) It is no surprise then that Talal Asad should claim that in the West, "belief is held to constitute the essence of 'religion'." (Asad 1996, 1–15, 11) The sheer bulk of Pelikan's documentary evidence, plus the testimony of conventional religious wisdom, gives ample testimony to this claim. Whether it be the Catholic or Reformed traditions, most Christians would accept Asad's view that for Christians it is "more important to have the right *belief* than to carry out specific prescribed practices." (Asad 1996, 1–15, 10) What is also remarkable is that this conventional wisdom of Western religion has, not surprisingly, shaped the way secular social scientists delimit the religious domain. Supporting the view that Western religious bias toward belief has infected more than religious discourse, but also shapes the way social scientists think about religion, is Asad's claim that one prominent modern anthropologist of his day, Clifford Geertz, exemplifies this way of conceiving religion as belief. Thus, Asad accuses Geertz of thinking that *belief* is some sort of basic ground of what is called 'religion,' since he says that "religious belief stands independently of the worldly conditions that produce" that with which we may connect it. For Asad, this is profoundly mistaken since beliefs change with the conditions in the world in which believers find themselves. (Asad 1993, 46) As for the scientific study of religion, it seems likewise significant that so influential a figure as former Harvard historian of religion Wilfrid Cantwell Smith falls prey to the same charge of identifying religion with *belief*. Smith's preferred term for conceiving religion is "faith," and as such, Smith's conception of religion can only be judged "pietistic" and "essentially individual and otherworldly." (Asad 2001, 205–22) Clearly, these are all terms that suggest that *belief* ("faith" by just another name) is the heart and soul of Smith's conception of religion.

We may quarrel about the precise date when people in the West started thinking about religion chiefly as belief, since Christians were laying out explicit statements of beliefs in their creeds from the early centuries. Yet, historian Benjamin J. Kaplan has argued that our particular modern stress on *belief* in its present form and with its attendant present strength came more recently in the pursuit of more recent theological strategies. Kaplan argues that religion in the West came to be identified with belief as late as the early modern period. This is not to deny the claim of an historian of equal eminence such as the late Jarolsav Pelikan that, at least for Christians, the command both to "believe" and to "confess" dates from the apostolic age. (Pelikan 2003) It is only to mark that the most recent emphasis and definition to this trend came in the wake of larger religious movements and their particular theological purposes. Thus, whether or not the early church's insistence upon formulating creedal statements of belief constituted the kind of extreme modern-day assumption we have that religion is chiefly and/or primarily about believing is not a question to which Pelikan addresses himself. Kaplan merely argues that the conditions set by the struggles over the Reformation intensified the insistence on a theological strategy in which belief became the ultimate criterion of religiousness. With Christendom divided, sides were taken in a pitted struggle against one another. Lines of loyalty had to be established with *precision*. In this way, Kaplan shows how religion came "increasingly to mean belief in a particular creed, and a life lived in accordance with it." (Kaplan 2007, 31) This is what Kaplan calls "confessionalism," the newly formed conviction in the West that beliefs *defined* the nature of religion. We thus are heir to a "form of religious culture that developed in the sixteenth and seventeenth centuries," with its attendant interests and strategies in tow, and which still dominates religion in the West to this day. (Kaplan 2007, 46)

b. Being religious means you must be ready to say so

Part of the 'confessionalist' project, or 'confessionalist strategy,' also means that religious beliefs are defined as being propositional. They are a "believing that." This is not to deny the frequent talk of belief in experiential or non-propositional terms, such as a trust or "believing in" (Jesus, for example). Accordingly, in their Manifesto of 2008 – itself a statement of essential *beliefs* – the Steering Committee of American Evangelicals says that what defines a real Evangelical Christian "above all else … is a commitment and devotion to the person and work of Jesus Christ. His teaching and way of life, and an enduring dedication to his lordship above all other earthly powers, allegiance, and loyalties." (Evangelical & Committee 2008, 1–20, 8) What is notable about the prestige of propositional belief is how even when featuring personal, experiential commitment – a "believing in" – the Evangelical community still reasserts the propositional nature of belief. Thus, the Evangelical Manifesto goes on to say that "being Evangelical means an ongoing commitment to Jesus Christ … to be Evangelical is to recognize the primacy of the authority of Scripture, which points us to Jesus …" (Evangelical & Committee 2008, 1–20, 10) It means that you must both *know* you are saved and be ready and rarin' to *say so*. Why it is so important that this kind of religiosity be pursued is scarcely, if ever, explored. It is simply self-evident.

But, in a particular case, what if *living* or merely *being* religious is really more important – from the point of view of eternity, for example!? What if the biblical injunction against so-called 'phariseeism' were heard more often? Matthew 7:21 is pretty clear on the subject: "Not everyone who says to me, 'Lord, Lord,' will enter the kingdom of heaven, but only he who does the will of my Father who is in heaven." What if there are a good deal more yawning gaps to be filled between the actuality of being religious and the idea of *confessing* so, or of *saying so* in lots of words:

> Thoughtful Christians will concede that, although theology has an essential function, theological discourse does not necessarily induce religious dispositions, and that, conversely, having religious dispositions does not necessarily depend on a clear-cut conception of the cosmic framework on the part of a religious actor. (Asad 1993, 36)

Living, on the one hand, and thinking or talking, on the other, are too often confused in the Western – "confessional" – notion of religion as belief. "It is a modern idea," adds Talal Asad, "that a practitioner cannot know how to live piously without being able to articulate that knowledge." (Asad 1993, 36) Confessionalism has made us all into OpEd (opinion page) pundits! So, a question for modern Christians – and, indeed, any religious people – might be what purposes such a construal of 'religion' entails. What purposes does it serve to pursue a religious strategy driven by the imperative of shouting one's beliefs from the rooftops? Likewise, what would a Christian 'religion' look like if it were to adopt another strategy – a strategy in which 'religion' was understood more humbly, more as a matter of *behaving* properly – more in the spirit of Matthew 7:21 – "only he who *does* the will of my Father" will enter the kingdom of the Father?

Especially when it comes to religion and public discourse, we need to realize what Asad is asserting here, since so much weight is often put on the *saying so* – on the fearless evangelical declaration of one's commitment or proud affirmation of one's being born-again. Although we talk a lot about anxieties over too much or too little religion in our political life, sometimes it is hard to know what the real problems are. To wit, is the problem the actual presence of religion in one form or another – anything ranging from personal religious motivation to explicit laws regulating or privileging a particular religion? Or is the problem one of publicizing one's religious affiliation, motivation, purposes, and so on – partly following a strategy dictated by the biblical imperative to preach the gospel to all nations? A remarkable recent document from a national committee of American Evangelicals, "An Evangelical Manifesto: A Declaration of Evangelical Identity and Public Commitment," at the very least suggests that saying so is something of a charged matter for some religious folk contemplating interventions into the public or political domains. Thus, they note boldly that "we affirm with the Apostle Paul that we are not ashamed of the gospel of Jesus Christ, for it is the power of God unto salvation." (Evangelical & Committee 2008, 1–20, 4) The pressure to 'confess,' to declare, to speak out – to *say so* – is palpable.

A recent 'flap' in British politics should drive my point home. Recently, it was reported in the *Los Angeles Times* that former British Prime Minister Tony Blair for the first time *declared* that "his faith has informed the essential backdrop to much of his political life." (Murphy 2008, A8) Blair had entered the modern territory of 'confessing,' of acting upon the religious imperatives assumed by the religion-is-belief crowd. In this case, Blair only recently announced his conversion to Roman Catholicism, "after years of secretly attending Mass" while prime minister, it was also reported. This admission bore special significance for some observers of the British political scene. In a remark unheard of in contemporary English, if not European, politics, Blair also told other reporters that he had "prayed while making his decision on committing British forces to Iraq." Similarly, it has been said by those close to Blair that his decisions on intervention in Kosovo and Sierra Leone as well were not "motivated" by some calculating political "practicalities," but by his belief that he was pursuing the "'right' thing to do." Spelling out the place of "faith" in his political life, Blair went on to say:

> Faith is not something separate from our reason, still less from society around us, but integral to it, giving the use of reason a purpose and society a soul, and human beings a sense of the divine ... This is the life purpose that cannot be found in constitutions, speeches, stirring art or rhetoric. It is a purpose uniquely centered around kneeling before God. (Murphy 2008, A8)

Were Blair's declaration the end of the story, little more would remain to say. But much more lies beneath the surface. Quite often, religion's being in the 'public square' is not so much whether or not someone's politics was actually motivated by religion, but that they should *confess* it – say so openly! Putting it rather uncharitably, one of Blair's irate critics, media commentator Ron Liddle, said: "'Tony believed in God but not with sufficient conviction or fervor to allow the voters to know he believed in God'." (Murphy 2008, A8) Once again, then, we meet the 'confessionalist' strategy in action: the depth of one's belief necessarily demands articulating it precisely, then shouting it from the rooftops! Some of the British public apparently feel that *'saying so'* matters a lot, arguably more than acting or living religiously.

Blair was quick to observe as much about his own country. For good or for ill, in the United States "open expressions of belief would not be unusual, in secular Europe ... religiosity tends to be viewed with suspicion." Of course, Blair does not broach the question of whether such a presumption that one should shout it out from the rooftops is a healthy matter for either religion or politics! In Britain, nevertheless, he thus deliberately hid public expression of his faith for fear of "being dismissed as a 'nutter'." (Murphy 2008, A8) In a similar vein, Blair noted how in Europe, "to admit to having faith leads to a whole series of suppositions, none of which are very helpful to the practicing politician." This led Blair's press secretary, Alastair Campbell, to dismiss public talk about religion in reporting memorably, "'We don't do God'." All this then raises the question of whether it is the possession of religious faith or membership in a religious body that causes the offense, or whether it is the publicity of being religious that does so.

This entire matter, of course, takes us into deeper questions about the psychology of belief. In particular, it raises skeptical questions about whether Blair can even be certain whether he was acting on his religious belief. Again, let us assume that Blair was sincere in *believing* that his religious convictions shaped his politics and policies. Fine. Yet, ever since Freud, can we be sure about the truth of claims to self-knowledge? A bit more humility about claims to perfect self-knowledge of our own motives, and their relation to our actions, might be in order. How, therefore, do we know – indeed how does Tony Blair himself know – that his political actions were indeed shaped by his religious beliefs? Self-delusion is a common enough occurrence; politicians are certainly not exempt – even those claiming religious motivation.

c. Religion as belief: A poor man's 'religion'

The implications of the 'confessionalist' strategy of reducing religion to belief, then, are many. While the precision of propositional statements might strengthen confessional discipline, a perhaps unintended consequence has been to devalue and eliminate much of the imaginative flair of poetry, myth, dance, and gesture from religion – and thus from a definition of 'religion.' Beliefs have to be precise. The kind of looseness characteristic of a flourishing interpretive fancy is intolerable. Some part of this lost world of the pre-confessionalist religious imaginary still survives to our day in pre-Reformation religious song. American composer Samuel Barber's settings of a cycle of "Hermit Songs," composed by Irish monks between the eighth and thirteenth centuries, captured this spirit well. They ravage the imagination with their wild and mysterious images. In "The Crucifixion," for example, the dying Jesus is addressed on the cross with strange words such as, "When they began to crucify you, Oh, Swan." What hints and mysteries lie in that epithet, "oh Swan"? In the "Heavenly Banquet," we find St. Brigid readying a massive beer 'blast' for Jesus:

> I would like a great lake of beer for the King of Kings.
> I would like to be watching Heaven's family
> Drinking it through all eternity.

What does this suggest about the life hereafter, especially if not taken prosaically, in earnest post-Reformation – 'confessional' – fashion as some spiritual 'matter of (doctrinal) fact'? More familiar, perhaps, are old Christmas carols still sung today, such as Robert Young's (1923) setting of the fifteenth-century "There Is No Rose of Such Virtue":

> There is no rose of such virtue as is the rose that bare Jesu;
> Alleluia.
> For in this rose contained was heaven and earth in little space.
> Res miranda [Wondrous thing!]
>
> By that rose we may well see that He is God in persons three,
> Pari forma [Of the same form!]

What splendid 'nonsense' – from the point of view of doctrinal rigor – to sing of Jesus having been given birth by a rose, or to sing of the rose revealing the triune God! But what sublime beauty, what joyous affection, what transcendent pleasure! But still, what literal 'nonsense' from the point of view of those who see religion as only a matter of having certain beliefs!

Even though we are here still in the world of discourse, albeit mythical and poetic discourse, it should be clear that a case has been made for the insufficiency of doctrines and beliefs to encompass the religious. I am arguing in this chapter that, if we wish, our concept of 'religion' could be *expanded* to include the poetic or mythical. So much of what passes as religious discourse is precisely of this mythical and poetic type, but these things are often not taken into

31

its definition. Given another vision, another set of purposes or strategies, they could be included in defining 'religion.' But that will wait upon theological innovation so to do. I have mentioned only some fragments of such songs. In the body of words spoken about religion and as 'religious,' the volume of mythical and poetic language is beyond counting. Defining religion, thus, in terms of belief is to impoverish the term 'religion' out of all recognition to what the whole weight of religious language alone contains. Perhaps some innovative theologian will re-conceive the purposes of the religious life to make the imagination and somatic part of that new life. This means, I think, that the concept of 'religion' could be vigorously *enriched, expanded,* or *reformed* to extend well beyond the soulless propositionalism or confessionalism of those who would reduce religion to a system of beliefs. Tragically, as I shall argue in my discussion of human bombers in the Middle East, the imaginative and somatic aspects of religion have served in the interests of violence – no matter how one might want to justify it or not. But, as I shall argue, it is only by reaching beyond religion-as-belief, religion-is-good, and other clichés that we can expect to engage politics in some way that reflects how things happen in a real world.

d. OMG!

But there's more to the Western bias toward defining religion in terms of belief – something one is tempted to call "Cliché 3 1/2." This is, of course, that for Western confessionalism religion is belief in God. That which many people still think defines religion, and *ought* to define it, is monotheism. A contemporary of Durkheim's, the Liberal Protestant Albert Réville, claimed that the notion that religious history brought "clearly into light the universality, the persistency and prodigious intensity of religion in human life, is therefore, to my mind, one unbroken attestation to God." (Réville 1905, 7) By this logic, "Cliché 3 1/2, Part B" reads that religion is internal experience of God – "a purely inner, private state of mind, a particular state of mind detached from everyday practices." (Asad 1996, 1–15, 10)

This viewpoint sometimes seems like a tune that can occur in several variations. Again, Albert Réville sings the praises of a natural psychological religious faculty, "an innate need of the human spirit." (Réville 1905, 6) His son, Jean Réville, waxed lyrical in saying that "the underlying and true explanation of religious phenomena" lay "in the imagination, heart, reason, conscience, instincts and passions" – all eminently interior, experiential aspects of human life. (Réville 1907, 189–207, 203) It would be an intriguing research enterprise to determine just what larger purposes defining 'religion' as the belief in a one God achieved. Given the number of monotheisms, and the vast number of their promoters, the answers will be many. I mean, even in Jean Bodin's great sixteenth-century debate on the nature of religion, *Colloquium of the Seven about Secrets of the Sublime,* the participants there concurred that the One God was the "Parent of all the gods" without *denying* that those who worshiped other or many 'gods' practiced a 'religion.' (Bodin 1975, 465) There, the Lutheran, Fridericus, flippantly poses the rhetorical question: "Who can doubt that the Christian religion is the true religion, or rather the only one?" Octavius, a Roman Catholic convert to Islam, is ready with an answer: "Almost all the world – Asia, large as it is, most of Africa, a great part of Europe – has infinite variety of sects, and each group thinks the religion which he especially loves is the most beautiful and noble." (Bodin 1975, 163) What particular purpose did the nineteenth-century promoters of monotheism and opponents of Durkheim then have for arguing their positions? What particular theological strategy was being fulfilled, and how would that have shaped the particular meaning of their definition of 'religion'?

6. 'Religion's' Private Parts

From the psychological and experiential nature of religion's essence, it follows that a fourth cliché attending the nature of religion flows – namely, that religion is necessarily *private.* On this view, 'real'

Christianity, like 'real' Islam, is 'interior' – things of personal morality or the 'heart' – something that can be discerned in a person by testing the quality of their sincerity, intentions, or beliefs. The assumption of such opposition between some autonomous interior redoubt and the profane world outside rests on some religious convictions particular to religious beliefs that grew out of the history of religion in the West. These remain today much taken for granted and very widespread, especially in the United States. Although this trend of religious thinking owes most to the Wesleyan tradition, its roots in the "religion of the heart," or the religion of sincerity and enthusiasm, run deeper into the groundwork of Western religious modernity. (Knox 1950) For the great nineteenth-century French Protestant theologian Auguste Sabatier, such eminently religious phenomena as "sin and expiation" are never *public,* but instead locked up securely and inviolably behind the shuttered doors "of the human heart." (Sabatier 1904, 134) This determination to define religion as private – and thus as autonomous of power, of any sort – leads thinkers imbued with the ideals of the privacy of religion into some odd views. If they meet undeniable public religious practices, such as ritual sacrifice, they find ingenious ways of negating their public character. Thus, Dutch historian of religion Cornelis P. Tiele affirmed that the only value in such a public religious display as a sacrificial ritual was the inner attitude of heart expressed there, the "yearning of the believer for abiding communion with" God. (Tiele 1898, 149) For thinkers like these, who dominated the study of religion for so long, key features of religion, such as sacrifice, were routinely interpreted in what they called 'spiritual' – and thus not public – terms. (Rivière 1912, 285, 98, 99)

While the idea of religion as involving intimacy is widely deployed across a host of religious traditions, the definition of religion in terms of its being something private and privileged has special roots in the determination of the Reformation to establish a special religious sensibility. To establish the so-called 'privacy' of religion is, on its other side, to make the same case as for its autonomy from politics and the 'public square.' Religion's privacy is rooted in Luther's larger politico-religious strategy of making the state "visible" by asserting its institutional independence from the Papal–Holy Roman Empire – from an ecclesiastical–imperial axis. "All coercive authority was vested in the prince by Divine Right; that the power of the State was absolutely vested in him; that no other separate organization could exist except by his fiat, or by his delegation … No real social unities are to exist apart from the State." (Figgis 1998, 69) The price to be paid for assertion of state autonomy was that religion would become 'invisible,' and autonomous in its own realm. Religion cedes the 'public square' to the political. Religion becomes something internal – a matter of the free, private conscience – without rights to a voice in the 'public square,' or it becomes contained within the institution of the national church. (Figgis 1998, 68) Religion, in the form of a social body, vacates the world of power and politics, and leaves the prince in charge over religion and the various state churches that grew up in post-Lutheran Europe.

7. Powerless in Paradise

Finally, and following immediately from the view that religion is an autonomous and private reality, is the common assumption that religion and power or politics have – historically speaking – had nothing to do with each other. Again, why anyone would assert this is baffling to anyone familiar with the history of the West alone. Were we to proceed by defining religion without any reference to power or politics, how would such a strategy of inquiry look? Writers like Talal Asad, Tim Fitzgerald, and others have offered answers to this question having to do with the establishment of a certain kind of modernity. But, for present purposes, it is enough here to recall that the Church of the Middle Ages was a thoroughly political body – in Colin Morris's words a "papal monarchy." (Morris 1989) Historian Judith Herrin, among others, notes that from the time of Charlemagne to the modern era "Christendom was also a polity in the West, not just a religious order." (Herrin 1987, 480) When the pope crowned Charlemagne, he not only legitimized the Carolingians as successors to the emperors of the West, but also and for the first time declared that the Church and the popes themselves were the "supreme political" authorities there as well. Historian John Neville Figgis claims that "The Holy Roman Empire ... did attempt to realize the idea of an all-powerful State, but that State was the Church." (Figgis 1998, 14) A mixture, then, of historical ignorance of the condition of medieval Christianity plus a revulsion for its marriage of religion and politics explains why our conventional wisdom today also dictates that religion and politics *should not* mix. When religion and politics get confused with one another, whatever is religious about religion, so to speak, gets destroyed in the process. The Mr. Dooley character, created by Finley Peter Dunne, rues the corruption of religion when the boundaries between it and politics are abolished: "Rellijon is a quare thing. Be itself it's all right. But sprinkle a little pollyticks into it an' dinnymit is bran flour compared with it." Better, says Dooley furthermore, that the realms of religion and politics be sealed off from one another: "Alone it [religion] prepares a man f'r a better life. Combined with polyticks it hurries him to it." (Kaplan 2007, 101) Such may still be our common conventional wisdom today that 'real' religion, so called, must have nothing political about it. People will decide on their own whether it is 'good' or 'bad' that religion should be defined as being either devoid of politics or potentially involved with it. We, at any rate, should at least put to rest the idea that religion can never be defined as having a political aspect. We can at least put aside the view that religion must *necessarily* be defined as an internal, disembodied private matter free of power or politics.

8. Two Ways to Eliminate 'Religion'

In response to this confusing clatter of clichéd definitions of 'religion,' a group of thinkers I call 'eliminationists' has found the challenge of our alternately ambiguous or narrow discourse about religion intolerable. Given such bad choices, these thinkers despair at talking about – or *with* – 'religion' at all. They range from those 'formalists' who imagine 'religion' a term empty of content, but useful as a contrast term to those 'reductionists' who would simply eliminate 'religion' from our vocabulary and substitute something else in its place. Formalists feel that because any *specific* content assigned to 'religion' is either too ambiguous or too narrow, the term should be regarded as "essentially empty, of use only as a marking device." (Braun 2000, 3–20, 9) To them, 'religion' names no objective thing alongside other things, with its own particular content. 'Religion' names no "substance that floats 'out there,' a something that might invade and enlighten us if we should be so fortunate as to have the right kind of receiving apparatus." 'Religion' is only the name of a logically 'formal' object. It is a "concept" – "something used to allocate the stuff of the real world into a class of objects … aimed toward explanation of their causes." (Braun 2000, 3–20, 9) Defining 'religion' is then an arbitrary sorting process – "as analogous to the manner in which the Library of Congress or British Library divides published material quite artificially among 'classes of conceptual and topical relations in the service of data retrieval'." (Braun 2000, 3–20, 10)

At the other extreme are those 'reductionists' who echo George Orwell's words about Newspeak's elimination of whole classes of words: "Countless other words such as honour, justice, morality, internationalism, democracy, science, and religion," says the despairing Winston Smith, "had simply ceased to exist." (Orwell 1948, 267–79) I call those who would purge 'religion' from our language 'eliminationists.' To them, we have no need of such a term, when others, like 'culture' or 'ideology,' would supposedly serve equally well or better. (Fitzgerald 1997, 91–110) For 'reductionists,' it may be immaterial whether religion is bad *or* good, private or public, and so on, because, for them, religion – in the sense of recognizably 'religious' beliefs, institutions, and such – just doesn't matter. Citing something called 'religion' as a cause of events in the world simply does not fulfill any defensible theoretical strategy, any effort to explain or understand things in the world. There is no fruitful intellectual strategy of understanding or explanation that would be advanced by reference to anything called 'religion.' Hence, there is no need for the concept 'religion' in understanding the world, since there is nothing in the world usefully named 'religion' that would help our understanding. One might just as well demand that the old pre-chemical idea of 'phlogiston' could help us understand nature today! What scientific strategy would that further? Natural scientists of an earlier age held that 'phlogiston' was one of the handful of basic elements in things which rendered them flammable, and which was released once things burst into flame. In an analogous way, some thinkers are felt to appeal to an idea like 'religion' – say in terms of *religious* motives – to account for why people do things in the world. Thus, some 'eliminationists' deny that people actually engage in "historical actions" out of "religious motives." (McCutcheon 2001, 2–3) Others believe that the term 'religion' "picks out nothing distinctive and it clarifies nothing" (Fitzgerald 1997, 91–110: 93) and, thus, that 'religion' is "virtually useless as a cross-cultural analytic concept." (Fitzgerald 1997, 91–110, 91) 'Religion' cannot serve any viable strategy for explaining the world. Like the budding 'chemists' of the nineteenth century, who wished to eliminate 'phlogiston' from the vocabulary of science, the eliminationists of 'religion' argue that there is no point in retaining or reforming 'religion.' We need to junk it.

But, of course, the real question for the reductionist of 'religion' is whether 'religion' is indeed our 'phlogiston,' whether strategies of explaining events in the world are furthered or hindered by employing a concept of 'religion.' But what if 'religion' is more like the equally old term 'science,' linked as it was with all sorts of occult practices and such, than like the term 'phlogiston'? 'Science' does not mean today what it meant for Isaac Newton, for example. Was Newton "the first scientist or the last magician," as John Maynard Keynes queried? Aside from 'science' being an ambiguous term covering anything in the realm of cognition, someone like Newton did not separate out the purposes and strategies of his so-called 'scientific' investigations from work we would call 'alchemical,' 'theological,' or even 'occultist.' Like what we would call 'religion' and 'politics' of that same bygone era, certain separations of purpose had not been effected. Yet, the term 'science' has been retained today, and the senses of it through the past can be linked with more or less success with those of our own day. Newton was surely doing something *like,* something *analogous* to, the 'science' of today, even if his wider purposes included the strategies of someone we would not recognize as a 'scientist.' What, then, if 'religion' is a term that can be similarly repaired and reformed, rather than eliminated? Answers to such questions are not obvious. Would we, for example, think as well that 'power' and 'politics' are like 'phlogiston' too? Ought they too be jettisoned, eliminated? Probably not. Are 'art,' 'morality,' 'the economy,' and others also like 'phlogiston'? Doubtless not, as well.

9. Is Religion Our Phlogiston? An Historical Test Case

A good test of whether religion is our phlogiston would be to submit this hypothesis to an empirical case-study. Some of our most eminent historians have nudged me in precisely the direction of more fully embracing religion as a factor in explaining the world, especially when issues of politics and power are concerned. As these historians show, attempts to eliminate religion from the understanding of certain historical periods simply fail to make sense of the world. Reducing religion to polity by leaving out notions like 'salvation' from the calculus of the French Wars of Religion turns out to obscure reality. Here, historian Mack Holt affirms the importance of the reality and concept of religion over against what can only be called 'mind boggling' efforts to *eliminate* religion from the equation. That Holt felt he had to write to defend the place of religion in – of all things – the French Wars of

Religion coincidentally testifies to the common prejudice against religion afflicting some quarters of academe. Says Holt:

> While I would be the first to agree that the politicization of religious issues played a significant role in shaping the course of the wars (especially during the wars of the League in the 1590s) and that socio-economic tensions were a permanent feature of early modern French society, occasionally bubbling over into popular violence, it seems to me that religion was nevertheless the fulcrum upon which the civil wars balanced. (Holt 1995, 1–2)

Some other sort of causal factor was at work, says Holt, in shaping the wars of religion than simply those of the "socio-economic" sort. A smarter explanatory strategy would find a way to include these.

Were Holt alone in having to deal with this tendency to eliminate religion from historical explanation, one might simply register his complaint as eccentric. But he is not. An equally distinguished historian, John Bossy, has been sharp in his criticism of historians who have written religion right out of 'what matters' in the study of modern politics. He too joins Mack Holt in excoriating eliminationist historians for effacing all mention of religion from an understanding of the wars of religion! "For a very long time," Bossy begins, "indeed to some degree ever since they occurred, it has been doubted whether Europe's wars of religion were actually religious wars." But this tendency was not limited to the perhaps understandable anti-clerical sentiments of Enlightenment Europe. Bossy continues:

> During the century or so in which modern historiography was establishing itself, one of the standard strategies of historical description was to explain that what appeared to be confessional conflicts in France, the Netherlands, Germany, England, or elsewhere, were actually political ones: something to do with the rise of the modern state. (Bossy 1991, 267–85, 268–9)

Unlike them, Bossy believes that political events have balanced on the "fulcrum" of religion. Bossy is accordingly 'amazed' that a historian of Calvin's Geneva, John Kelley, would leave out entirely the category of "church" from his book on the consolidation of French Protestantism! (Bossy 1991, 267–85, 277) For these modern historians, then, "people do not really fight about religion. If they seem to be doing so, they must really be fighting about something else." (Bossy 1991, 267–85, 278) Why anyone would actually think such counterintuitive things leaves one to puzzle about the anti-religious prejudices that often emerge among some of our colleagues in the university. Bossy confirms such suspicions directly, and offers an explanation of them. Those colleagues are obsessed by alternative categorization – especially with 'power' and 'politics,' as their liberationist leanings would prefer.

These obsessions have produced a bitterly ironic result. Despite the liberationist commitments to a grassroots history, these elimina-tionists have imposed upon the grassroots an entirely modern con-ception of the world. Despite their often passionate desire to offer a 'history' that gave voice to the previously voiceless, these liberation-ist histories of the wars of religion have simply ridden roughshod over the "natives' point of view." Here is Bossy on this point:

> The language in which what might seem to be religious conflict was described, often enough by participants as well as by their inter-viewers from the media was the language of liberation, revolution, and their opposites, of left and right. It seemed unsophisticated, improper, and sometimes against the law to refer to these things by the names that most naturally came to mind. Lebanese Christians and Muslims were referred to respectively, as right-wingers and left-wingers; in Northern Ireland, the Social Democratic and Labor Party or SDLP was a political party concerned with human rights whose voters just happened, as the BBC grudgingly conceded, to be "mainly Catholic." (Bossy 1991, 267–85, 268)

Thus, while the historians Bossy criticized may have succeeded in shifting attention from the 'Great Men' of state, from their acts of regal diplomacy and statecraft, and refocused attention onto ordi-nary people, they *eliminated* the religion of ordinary folk at the same time! Instead, they impose their own ideology, their own hegemonic intellectual strategy, upon early modern Europeans, and simply reveal the prejudices of our own time and place.

A great deal of damage has been done to our understanding of world-critical events, because these reductionist histories have produced "'categorical anachronism'." The terms in which the wars of religion have been discussed and explained are done so in language that would not even be recognized by the participants. And, without at least some recognition – not 'acceptance' – of the worldview of the participants it is unlikely that our explanatory strategies can succeed. (Taylor 1985b, 116–33) Such histories, in short, confuse the purposes people may be pursuing. They confuse "matters of polity with matters of salvation" – politics and religion – when they are not running any sort of religious strategy right out of the picture entirely. A demand for 'recognition' in no way should be seen as any sort of demand for approval of the descriptions or explanations of the events in the wars of religion, or of the intellectual purposes of the actors in it. The ideal of 'recognition' simply requires us to attend to the notions that would make sense to our subjects and resist making 'them' another step up the ladder of a brilliant career. Bossy can point proudly to some of the finest historians of the period, such as Natalie Zemon Davis or Benjamin Nelson, as exemplary historians who work with the categories that the subjects of their history would 'recognize.' Both, therefore, resist "'categorical anachronism'" by avoiding the use of terms that simply do not fit the mindset of the actors in the historical dramas of early modern Europe. (Davis 1975; Nelson 1969)

10. Talal Asad's 'Religion' Trouble

No discussion of the category 'religion' would be complete without attention to the most prominent and sophisticated critic of that term, anthropologist Talal Asad. One hesitates in calling Asad an outright eliminationist in part because Asad is by far the most elusive critic of the idea of religion on the current scene. Consider what seems a rather hard-edged advocacy of the elimination of 'religion.' Asad applauds it as "truly original" that historian of religion Wilfrid Cantwell Smith denies that religion "has any essence." Along with Smith, Asad declares further that "religion" names nothing 'objective' in our world. (Asad 2001, 205–22, 206) With Smith again, Asad says that 'religion' names no universal phenomenon of human life: "we have to abandon the idea of religion as always and essentially the same …" (Asad 2001, 205–22, 220) Such statements as these seem to leave little doubt that Asad takes his place alongside those reductionist eliminationist historians so heavily attacked by Mark Holt and John Bossy.

But I would give a false impression if I were to leave matters there, since, by any measure, Asad writes constantly and *uncritically* about what passes as 'religion' in common speech – Islam, Christianity, Judaism, and such. Moreover, he writes generally about 'religion' constantly and *uncritically* to address matters of "modern religion in Europe," or a "former kind of religiosity" or "forms of religiosity," or "the development of religions" or "essential religious virtue," and so on. (Asad 1996, 1–15, 11) The puzzle for interpreters of Asad remains, therefore, how to put together what seems like elimination of 'religion' with a continuation of its use – a rejection of a universal, cross-cultural comparative category, but the regular and general use of the same notion? What really is Asad rejecting when he rejects 'religion,' but persists in using the term to pick out examples of the object of his studies of 'religion'? What does Asad mean – really – when he declares that "we have to abandon the idea of religion as always and essentially the same …"? (Asad 2001, 205–22, 220) Does *he* use one set of criteria for selecting a 'religion' in one case, and other criteria in another?

While Asad's ultimate attitude toward 'religion' may be problematic, it is at least clear that Asad surely means that we need to abandon obviously parochial notions of 'religion.' Here, I join forces with Asad in calling attention to those concepts of 'religion' that are part of the theological purposes and strategies of missionaries – for example, some of the six clichés already mentioned. Asad surely means to deny the putative universality of the so-called 'liberal Protestant' or 'confessional' idea of religion – as belief and as "a purely inner, private state of mind, a particular state of mind detached from everyday practices." (Asad 1996, 1–15, 10ff.) If *that* is *really* what Asad means by 'religion,' then one can hardly argue with his criticisms just outlined. Here, I believe, some of Asad's own life story may help us understand his fierce objection to this 'liberal Protestant' idea of religion that he assigns to anthropologist Clifford Geertz. (Asad 1993, 48) In an account of his schooling by Christian missionaries in Pakistan, Asad makes a special point of recounting the humiliating experiences he had as schoolboy at the hands of Christian missionaries and their attitudes toward 'religion.' One can only imagine how a young Muslim boy of tender dispositions would react to a view of 'religion' that made little of his own Muslim religious life. This sort of Western missionary is known to make out that their ways of being religious were the only, or most exalted, form of being religious. In cases like that, justifiable resentment is sure to follow. "Well, if *that* is what religion is, then I reject *'religion'!*" (Scott 2006, 243–303) Thus, when Asad argues against Geertz in his classic of 1993, *Genealogies of Religion,* and repeatedly in other works, that "a transhistorical definition of religion is not viable," it is surely what I have called the 'liberal Protestant' idea of 'religion,' housed as it was in a strategy of fulfilling the purposes of conversion from Islam, that Asad eliminates as a cross-culturally comparative category. (Asad 1993, 30) Although treading into the psychological territory of the motivations behind a thinker's ideas can be treacherous, in Asad's case it seems to me to offer a plausible interpretive context all the better to grasp his critiques of 'religion.' After all, the (presumably liberal) Protestant missionaries of Asad's youth do think about religion in the universal, autonomous, belief-centered way that Asad attacks, integral to their colonial missionary purposes as well!

The problem is, however, that Asad seems to press eliminationism nonetheless. As recently as 2003, Asad reinforced this dismissal of the 'liberal Protestant' idea of 'religion' from any role in making sense of what people do because "there is nothing essentially religious, nor any universal essence that defines 'sacred' language or 'sacred' experience." (Asad 2003, 25) Such a statement, however, does not jibe with Asad's desire in the same essay to assert that "the meanings of religious practices and utterances … are to be explained as products of historically distinctive disciplines and forces." (Asad 1993, 54) If there is nothing essentially religious, or even, for that matter, distinctively or arguably religious, how does Asad decide what to indicate as an example of "religious practices or utterances"? So, Asad cannot altogether mean what he seems to be saying in saying that "there is nothing *essentially* religious." If Asad means anything consistently, he must only mean to criticize uses of 'religious' in the 'confessional' or 'liberal Protestant' idea of religion as belief.

It seems as well obvious that if we eliminate *any* notion of 'religion' as some of Asad's words sometime indicate, then we will have great difficulty making sense of such things as 9/11 — or so I shall argue in my concluding chapter on so-called Muslim 'suicide bombers.' Unlike Asad, I have no difficulty arguing that some religious purposes or strategies are *analogously linked* across time and cultures. In my view the human bombers of 9/11 performed sacrificial *'religious' acts* in a sense *analogous* to the ritual sacrifice of animals at the *Hajj,* or the intended sacrifice of Ishmael by Abraham as depicted in the Quran, for example. If it would impoverish our understanding of Isaac Newton to refuse to call his thinking 'science,' then it would impoverish our understanding of human cultures, and especially of politics *and* religion, if we could not speak of the acts of the human bombers of 9/11 as 'religious.' That at least is a major argument of this book, and where I take most exception to the contrary views of Asad. I do not think we need to wind up like the users of Newspeak satirized by George Orwell, for whom "Countless other words such as *honour, justice, morality, internationalism, democracy, science,* and *religion* had simply ceased to exist." (Orwell 1948, 267–79) Of course, if Asad only means to reject 'religion' in the sense of its being equated with its 'confessional' use, there is every reason to applaud him. Indeed, I shall be pleased to cite Asad frequently and favorably in this book for his elegant assertion of religion as involving "embodied practices," or for his salutary conception of religion as consisting in "networks of emotional connection." (Asad 1996, 1–15; 2005, 12)

At least implicitly, then, I think Asad can be read as advancing a project of expanding our notions of religion by overcoming biases against contextualization of the notion, and in favor of belief and asserting the proper place of emotions, body, and power. No reason to argue with that. But no reason *not* to call that 'religion' as well. We can, thus, be comfortable with Asad's writing of the possibility of a different "kind of religiosity" than that preferred by the tendencies inherent in the biases dictated by the history of West. (Asad 1996, 1–15, 11) We have much to gain, as I shall show, from incorporating his investigations into what he calls "prescribed moral-religious capabilities, which involve the cultivation of certain bodily attitudes (including emotions) the disciplined cultivation of habits, aspirations, desires," and so on. (Asad 1996, 1–15, 11) We have much to gain, as I shall again show, in joining forces with Asad in targeting for 'elimination' – or at least for serious reform – the disembodied, over-intellectualized conception of religion as 'belief.' We too seek to think about developing another "kind of religiosity." And, if that is so, then given a certain *purpose* to our inquiries, given a certain intellectual *strategy,* we might want to ask what that other "kind of religiosity" might have to do with politics. In part, this is what I shall be doing throughout this book, since I find that Asad's attack on dominance in many quarters of the 'liberal Protestant' idea of religion is generally on target. It qualified, as one should recall, as one of my 'six clichés' about the meaning of 'religion.'

11. The Trick of Defining 'Religion'

Now, as I have suggested, I think the eliminationists of whatever species are in key aspects wrong. But how, then, do I address the concerns of people fed up with the frustrations of defining 'religion'?

How might one make a case that 'religion' is a serviceable concept, a notion definable in some appropriate way, rather than eliminated or reduced to an empty form? How as well do we get beyond the positivism of today's social sciences – beyond those people who would, in effect, just open the Yellow Pages to the section entitled 'religion' and define 'religion' in terms of what one finds there? Better yet, how do we get past those in the university who would similarly scan the indices of most of our behavioral and social science publications or academic courses, and see what turns up under 'religion'? Political scientists, sociologists, social psychologists, criminologists, most anthropologists (Asad and Geertz being notable exceptions), and so on take the term 'religion' 'off the shelf' so to speak. Partly because of the positivist epistemological standards of 'social research,' they rarely, if ever, move beyond the commonsense uses of the term 'religion' to deeper criticism of them. As I shall argue shortly, positivism fails as an intellectual basis for conceptual thinking because it does not *take responsibility* for its concepts. It mindlessly just selects whatever carries the name 'religion' and proceeds from there. But how do those doing so know that the term 'religion' means the same for the items selected in this way? They cannot. We may reject unacceptable clichés about 'religion' or even eliminate 'religion' altogether from our language. But *rejecting* ideas about what we should mean by 'religion' does not excuse us of offering something that makes better sense. Therefore, we cannot escape the task of critically coming to terms with the definition of religion.

This chapter will conclude by articulating an approach to the definition of religion that has the following seven characteristics of the definition of 'religion' thus derived.

a. Pragmatic: Useful for explanation

First, when I say that the concept of religion should be defined *pragmatically,* I mean that we should submit the term to a test of its utility. Does a particular use of 'religion' help us understand the world, or not? Does it add anything otherwise missing? Thus, even as I think the formalists are partially correct in saying that they would have us see 'religion' as "marking" certain things in the world, they provide no answer to the question of how this is to be done short of assigning 'religion' some sort of distinctive – not autonomous – *content*. And, if at some point we need to truck with *content,* and not just formal functioning, we need to get into the messy business of definition.

b. Distinctive: The definition must offer a 'distinctive' concept of what religion is

Second, part of the trick to defining 'religion' comes, in part, in making a case that the content assigned to 'religion' is *distinctive or different enough* to merit there being such a notion at all. The concept of 'religion' then does not require that religion be an absolutely unique, incomparable, or 'autonomous' reality. That the content is different enough or distinctive comes, in turn, as I shall argue, from attention to the context of inquiry, to our strategies and purposes.

c. Not defined in the abstract

Third, I do not think there is any answer to the question of the definition of 'religion' in the *abstract*. In what *context* do we propose to use the word 'religion'? Such a content is thus not determined by some *abstract* criteria, e.g. neither too narrow nor too broad, nor, again, too formal or not. I propose that we define 'religion' *relatively* and *contextually*. That is to say, 'religion' will in part be defined with respect to different purposes, strategies, contexts of argument, and so on.

d. Not formalistic or artificial

Fourth, therefore, while the act of defining 'religion' is a *constructive* one, it is not as 'artificial' as the formalists would have it. The definition of 'religion' does not fall from the sky; it is not an abstract isolate. Rather, in defining 'religion,' we do so as part of a larger effort at thinking – something that can be called a 'strategy' behind our thought. The final chapter of this book – on the 'religion' in human bombing, so to speak – is offered as a test of the utility of my proposal for defining 'religion' with respect to our different purposes, strategies, contexts of argument, and so on.

e. Accurate, not necessarily precise

Fifth, I also approach definition in a rather more 'relaxed' way. A definition of 'religion' needs to be *'accurate,'* but not technically be *'precise.'* When it comes to 'religion' we are not required to be more precise, rigorous, stringent, and so on about defining religion than we are when we speak of any other major category of thought – 'power' and 'politics' included. As anthropologist Louis Dumont said of 'power,' for instance, "'Power' is a notion which, while playing a central role in contemporary political science, is so obscure that it has scarcely justified this role." (Dumont 1979, 165)

f. Relative to contexts, strategies and purposes

Sixth, the logical consequence of my proposing that the definition of religion should *not* be independent of use, abstract, formalistic, arbitrarily precise is that religion *should* be defined in relation to our larger intellectual *purposes, strategies,* and such. It is the sixth element of the definition of 'religion' that accounts for both accuracy and precision – the contexts, strategies, and purposes driving our interests.

g. In touch with commonsense

Seventh, a defensible point of departure would involve beginning with *everyday speech and commonsense,* but not ending there. If 'religion,' which is after all a term from *everyday speech,* names *anything* – if it *refers* to *anything* – then it refers to something close to a system of beliefs and practices, revolving about sacred or transcendent beings or states, expressed in and formed by characteristic myths, doctrines, moral systems, social organizations, psychological states, and material forms, that bespeak ultimate authority in human affairs. That is, at least, what an 'informed' commonsense, chastened by an awareness of prevailing clichés, tells us 'religion' means in ordinary language. If we thus take our departure from such a definition, it, at least, lets us locate the rough coordinates of the object of our discourse in everyday parlance. Even Asad, with his will to eliminate or seriously curtail use of the term 'religion,' in practice adopts much the same approach, as I have shown. If there is nothing 'essentially' religious, as he says, or even for that matter, distinctively or arguably religious, how does Asad even decide what to indicate as an example of "religious practices or utterances"? Asad leans on everyday speech, even if he never says this.

But, while commonsense understandings of 'religion' in ordinary language may make a reasonable enough place to begin, critical thinking never stops at commonsense, never is content with ordinary language. Given all the difficulties we have registered with the confusing or clichéd uses of 'religion' and with efforts to eliminate or 'reduce' it, no critical thinker can be satisfied with commonsense. A thinker seeking to be more *accurate* about their thinking about 'religion' will need to press past the commonsense of everyday usage. In the end, we have no other choice than to try to be critical of commonsense notions of 'religion' or to *refine* them, so to speak. But, just how do we take the next step beyond commonsense? How do we do something that could be called *refining* our definitions of 'religion'?

12. Owning 'Religion'

Refining our definitions of 'religion' quite simply means that we, 'critical thinkers,' need to seize the initiative and make some conceptual *decisions*. This means that the way we *refine* commonsense definitions of 'religion' is not by searching for some objective 'genuine' or 'authentic' religion 'out there' that might serve as 'gold standard' of reference of the term, 'religion.' The name 'religion' can be applied to all sorts of things, as we have seen. There is no 'objective,' uncontestable, referent to the term 'religion' which could settle our problems of definition. In this regard, I share with the 'formalists' the view that 'religion' names no objective thing alongside other things – no "substance that floats 'out there,' a something that might invade and enlighten us if we should be so fortunate as to have the right kind of receiving apparatus." (Braun 2000, 3–20, 9) However, as I argued as well, it makes no good critical sense to use the term 'religion' in this 'formalist' way. From the point of view of the operation of "marking" that the formalist approach proposes, *any* term would do to 'mark' a distinction between one thing in the world from another. There must be some reason to call some things 'religion' rather than not. That is why I prefer to begin by admitting the reality of our everyday language and the commonsense notions of religion it contains. Everyday usage at least proposes a *content* – albeit a *content* requiring *refinement,* criticism, and so on – that proposes to distinguish religion from other bits of our intellectual universe. And here is where the element of conceptual *decision and choice* inevitably enters.

In this book, I propose to define 'religion' partly in terms that fit the theoretical *purposes or strategies* that I have chosen or assumed. At the risk of jumping ahead of myself, let me just say that in the case of the Middle Eastern human bombers in the final chapter, I have fixed on the notion of *authority* as *distinctively* marking their 'religious' character – in addition to the whole complex one calls 'Islam.' I select the notion of authority (*auctoritas*) because it offers a way of pointing out features often overlooked or ignored in dealing with events in our world that are apparently ones of religion and politics. That is to say that while both power, proper – *potestas* – and authority – *auctoritas* – can be found in all sorts of social formations, whether these be politics, religion, the arts, and so on, a fruitful way to distinguish religion and politics would be along lines following a particular distinction between *potestas* and *auctoritas*. Thus, I refer to the following formula to mark an accurate, pragmatic, distinctive content of the term 'religion,' relative to the context of the world of religion and politics: while a given 'religion' may display both *potestas* and *auctoritas,* no 'religion' is conceivable without *auctoritas*. Yet, some religions are conceivable in the absence of *potestas*. But, on the other hand, while politics too reveals a mixture of both *potestas* and *auctoritas,* it is conceivable without *auctoritas,* but no political entity lacking *potestas* is conceivable. While elements of this definition are well rooted in everyday notions of religion, I think the definition takes us beyond mere recycling of everyday understandings of religion. It puts the notion of authority forward – ultimate, sacred, and transcendent authority, to be precise. In terms of the purposes and strategies confronting me, the notion of authority will prove itself to be a useful way to shed light on at least one case where religion and politics are at play.

Actually, I think everyone seeking to think about religion in some critical or rigorous way does something of the same sort of choosing among possible elements distinguishing what 'religion' is in the cases they address. The only difference between them and me is that I admit, indeed embrace, the element of choice or decision dictating how I define 'religion.' I, therefore, doubt that 'religion' is ever really defined or used *in the abstract*. The decisions we make for defining 'religion' are conditioned by the larger theoretical strategies and interest we have in place – whether we care to admit them or not. In my discussion of the 'religion' in human bombing, so to speak, I am pleased, therefore, to declare that my *choice* of 'authority' as a *distinguishing* feature of their 'religious' character depends on the larger, encompassing theoretical strategy I pursue in seeking to engage the differences between 'religion' 'power,' and 'politics.' After the discussion of this chapter on 'religion,' I should hope that many of us will realize that 'religion' can mean many things. Those enlightened by my arguments here will, I hope, realize as well that 'religion' is not a term dropped from the heavens, nor that our commonsense conceptions of 'religion' are adequate to all tasks. As a result, in practice, when we speak of 'religion,' we opt for one or a range of definitions rather than others. We choose. We decide. We discriminate – whether consciously or not. We stress certain aspects of a commonsense definition of religion rather than others, as I have shown in my treatment of the six clichés. When I take up the matter of human bombers in the Middle East, I shall show how my use – and thus refined definition – of the term 'religion' is to be found in my larger polemic and intellectual projects, strategies, or purposes.

But what do I mean when I say I am adopting an approach to the definition of 'religion' that assumes a vital role for choice and decision regarding the *'strategic'* dimension in inquiry? How one defines 'religion' results in part from an engagement with a set of purposes or issues. I do not believe that we can or should define 'religion' in the abstract. Since I only *start* with a commonsense, working definition of 'religion' to get things going, at some point I need to accept *responsibility* for my categories of inquiry. Everyday or commonsense usage speaks in many tongues; it makes no discriminations. Thus, at some point, even if we stay close to commonsense everyday usage, we need to say what *elements* of that usage we take to be salient or *definitive*. What part of the everyday, commonsense definition of 'religion' do I *own?* When we think about religion, we necessarily decide among those meanings which we will *own.* Think, for example, about someone writing a book about 'art' or the 'art scene' in early 1900s Paris. They might simply report upon whatever passed in common parlance as 'art' – but without ever pressing the speakers about what 'art' meant. Ordinary usage would be the standard by which the referents to the word would be determined. A painting by Degas is 'art,' as is a sculpture by Rodin, and so on. But what if this book left out those rarities who had mastered the 'art' of living, or the *danseuse* for whom all was 'art'? They were not 'art,' only the work of a Degas or Rodin was 'art.' But who decides? That is the point precisely. Someone decides, and for some reason. When and if we decide to include Degas but to exclude our free-spirited *danseuse,* as well we might, we are *taking responsibility* for a concept of 'art.' Assuming *responsibility* for a concept, a definition of 'art' in this case, does not imply defining it *correctly* or not. It merely puts on record a decision about the purposes and strategies of our thinking.

Although this process of accepting *responsibility* or *ownership* for a definition of 'religion' has hardly been recognized as such, it is actually quite old. It is at least as old a process with as long a history as Jean Bodin's (1529–1596) famous *Colloquium of the Seven about Secrets of the Sublime* (1588). Bodin used the word 'religion' in a variety of ways readily understandable to us. There were "true," "false," "best," "oldest," "accepted," or "approved" 'religions.' Bodin's *Colloquium* also spoke of pagan, Christian, Jewish, and "Mohammedan" 'religions' – all contrasted with sorcery. And, as Quentin Skinner notes (to Fitzgerald's chagrin), there is even a stout defense in the *Colloquium* against compelling religion – as 'belief.' (Fitzgerald 2007, 150; Skinner 1978, 249) But Bodin was not satisfied with this riot of uses – uses proper to the *commonsense* of his time. At a certain point, in pursuit of what he took to be the 'truth' about the nature of religion, Bodin took ownership of a notion of 'religion.' When pressed to identify a decisive element in the 'religions' that got to the heart of what a 'religion' was, Bodin argued that this was the notion of the one God as the "Parent of all the gods." In effect, although all the 'religions' mentioned were still valid examples of 'religion,' like different musical notes on the scale, true 'religion' in the end required a 'harmony' among these 'notes.' Harmony could only be achieved by way of resolution of diversity into the unity of monotheism. (Bodin 1975, 465) Why Bodin pressed this intellectual strategy of an analogy between the 'religions' and music suggests a larger perspective that in turn harmonizes with his interests in Hermeticism and its grand view of a harmonious cosmos. Unresolved for me, for example, was how Bodin's conclusion that the "best" religion was the "oldest" – and hence presumptively, Judaism – fit with his Hermetic views. We know that Bodin was at least suspected of being a "Judaizer" and perhaps a crypto-Jew. This explains why he thought that the oldest religion was most likely to be the true religion, even if it leaves in question the relation of such a view to his ideas of cosmic harmonies. (Bodin 1975, 173)

13. How Durkheim Took 'Ownership' of 'Religion'

Closer to our time, we can see more clearly how the larger purposes of inquiry also played their roles in setting a definition in place – here by the negative process of *defining* something as non-'religion.' When, for example, Christian missionaries approached Theravāda Buddhism, they came to it with a particular interest of converting Buddhists to Christianity. They, of course, also came ready with their own definition of 'religion' as something related to a belief in God. Part of missionary strategy was to discredit – *disown* – Theravāda Buddhism by defining it as something inferior (in their minds) to what Christianity was – *not* a 'religion.' Theravāda Buddhism was thus 'defined' as a human creation – a 'philosophy,' and excluded from the class of objects known as 'religions.' In the minds of missionaries, the only definition of 'religion' worthy of *ownership* had to be something, to them, 'higher' – God-given and God-related. Thus, the definition of 'religion,' and more to the point, the definition of Theravāda Buddhism as not-a-'religion' can be seen as part of a way to fulfill certain *strategic* missionary purposes. Theravāda Buddhism was not a 'philosophy' in *abstraction,* but only in *relation* to Christian missionary interests and purposes. I am seeking to embrace this perspective on the definition of religion in this book.

In this, I follow the example of Durkheim's inclusion of Theravāda Buddhism in the class of objects called 'religions.' I am arguing that because he brought quite a different set of interests and strategies to Theravāda Buddhism, he defined it in quite a different way from the missionaries. For this reason we should not see Durkheim's definition of 'religion' without reference to belief in any god as something that 'fell from the sky' or was something done abstractly.

Durkheim's definition of 'religion' in the absence of a belief in God was not some arbitrary choice on his part. His interests and strategies were deeply involved. It was thus not accidental that Durkheim had been struggling to establish his sociological approach to religion in a place and time where mainly theological definitions prevailed. Part of Durkheim's purpose in defining 'religion' without reference to belief in God was intellectually grounded in his effort to unseat the Liberal Protestant theologians who dominated the study of religion in his day. (Strenski 2003b) These are, of course, the same kind of Christian who would have ruled Theravāda Buddhism not a 'religion.'

Part of Durkheim's strategy was to undermine the hegemonic power of the definition of certain words – like 'religion' – ones that aided the theologians in maintaining their preeminence in the study of religion. As someone who sought a 'scientific' study of religion and who opposed theological approaches to religion, Durkheim was convinced that this meant that key terms in the study of religion needed to be 'neutral' as to confessional character. In defining 'religion' as belief in God, Durkheim felt that the theologians had violated this 'scientific' neutrality – in favor of the theism central to the theological position held by his rivals, the theologians. To achieve that strategic end, Durkheim *defined* religion differently. He defined 'religion' such that the idea of belief in God no longer held hegemonic sway. For Durkheim, 'religion' was defined more inclusively by making the fundamental element in it the idea of the *'sacred.'* At one stroke, this permitted Durkheim to encompass things like Christianity within his definition of 'religion' – but significantly, also, something atheistic, like Theravāda Buddhism, which the Liberal Protestant theologians and their missionizing brethren defined otherwise.

Now, what I must underline here is the creative, theoretical strategic character of Durkheim's act of deciding to call Theravāda Buddhism a 'religion.' It is not as if Durkheim looked out on the world and noticed that some things – say Theravāda Buddhism – came with the label 'religion' slapped on them, but had inexplicably

56

been excluded from the list of 'religions.' No. Durkheim himself applied the label 'religion' to Theravāda Buddhism, as it were, in order to help fulfill his own theoretical strategies. He declared it a member 'in good standing' of the class 'religion' because doing so satisfied the larger purposes he wished to fulfill in his thinking about the whole of human society. Durkheim took the risks of accepting 'ownership.'

Informed by this larger strategic vision, Durkheim argued that the idea of the 'sacred' provided a richer, more defensible content to the idea of 'religion' than belief in God. Durkheim believed this because he believed that humans needed something more to flourish than 'bread alone,' so to speak. They needed things one might only call 'spiritual' – morality, inspiration, meaning, the stuff of the traditional religions – even the 'atheistic' ones like Theravāda Buddhism. But if, as Durkheim thought in his time, these age-old religions were vanishing, then what hope had the human prospect? None, unless we could either find or create things that fulfilled the same, or *analogous,* functions that the old religions had done. This core idea of the sacred enabled Durkheim to speak of the evolution of religions from traditional ones, like Christianity or Islam, to those that Durkheim foresaw succeeding them in the future – a religious humanism, individualism, or nationalism, for example. The common element shared all along the trajectory of religious evolution was the sacred. It was to be found, Durkheim believed, in all things commonly called 'religions.' In humanism and individualism, the human person is a 'sacred' being. Our bodies, our privacy, our consciences, our freedoms and rights are inviolable – sacred – and not to be transgressed. Even Buddhism, despite its atheism, regarded key things as sacred. Thus, Buddhism *compares* well with Christian or Hindu 'religions,' in possessing a tradition of institutionalized monasticism in which certain central vows are considered sacred, for example. Beyond the sacred, does not Buddhism, as well, reveal other features typical of 'religions' – a *comparatively* rich ritual life, like Christianity, Hinduism, or anything else one might want to call 'religion'? Does it not, furthermore, orient its members toward something that *compares well* with what might be called the 'transcendence' found in other things that we call 'religions'? Ought not all these features of 'religion' go to make up a definition of 'religion,' rather than just the belief in God? The upshot of this challenge, then, is that the definition of 'religion' developed by Durkheim originates in a strategy worked out in his entire approach to religion.

Much the same process of definition following strategic purpose prevails in other domains of culture. Religion is not peculiar in this respect. Consider again an example from the world of the arts. Despite the historicity and cultural specificity of notions like 'art,' the history of art in the West in the twentieth century teaches us that reformations and revolutions in our basic categories ought to be thought commonplace. When, in 1917, Marcel Duchamp's "Fountain" (actually a public lavatory urinal) was placed in a Paris gallery show, the entire art world and its public were scandalized. Was this 'art' or an adolescent effort to shock the *bien pensant* public? Yet, as demonstrating Duchamp's conception that the notion of 'art' could – and should – be challenged, Duchamp enriched and enhanced the concept. It was an extraordinary achievement on the epistemological level alone. Duchamp was doing many things besides merely defying the bourgeois 'art' public. He was teaching them something new. Duchamp was, in effect, demonstrating that the mere act of 'placing' or 'framing' of commonplace, even vulgar and utilitarian things – *"objets trouvées"* ('found objects') or 'ready-mades' – within a certain context could force a new classification as 'art.'

Additionally, the "Fountain" pushed the proposition of the decisive nature of 'framing' to the limits. Along the way, it created a new definition of art. But, strategically, that is what Duchamp wanted to do. The "Fountain" was not a 'one off' – not an isolated creation – but like Durkheim's 'placing' of the 'sacred' at the center of the definition of 'religion,' part of a strategy for remaking our categories. If the "Fountain" passed as 'art,' anything could, so long as it was 'framed' within the appropriate context. If Theravāda

Buddhism passed as 'religion,' then other comparable atheistic systems embodying the sacred could as well. This also opened the door for followers of Durkheim to see humanism, individualism, nationalism, or notoriously, fascism, as 'religions' or 'religious.' (Gentile 1996; Ranulf 1939, 16–34) Duchamp's genius was thus to call attention to the conventional definition of 'art,' and then to challenge it. His role was to confront that conventional definition and challenge it in the same way that Durkheim's different appreciation of Buddhism challenged the theistic definition of 'religion.' What we had hitherto thought was only peripheral to 'art' – the framing, the staging, and so on – like what some had thought to be only peripheral to religion – the ritual, the division of sacred space and time, and so on – turn out to be central to their definition. In Duchamp's world, the definition of 'art' drifted or grew, as tastes would have it. In our world, the definition of 'religion' can likewise be more 'relaxed' and more self-consciously defined in terms of a theoretical *strategy*.

14. Religion and Its Despisers

The view I am elaborating in this chapter is that 'religion' is still the serviceable name for a set of purposes or life strategies, but one needing a good deal of *reforming*. Appealing to 'religion' and 'religious' strategies likewise makes for a serviceable way of making sense of the world. My decision to retain 'religion,' then, reflects the sense that there is something that can be picked out in the world and usefully named 'religion.' As I argue in the concluding chapter on suicide bombings in the Middle East, religious purposes may even be more prominent than in the recent past. While it has been our unthinking habit too easily to equate 'religion' with faith or belief, I shall argue that both here and abroad, there is far more to 'religious' purposes than that. The 'more' is, in turn, responsible for why religion is becoming a greater force in our world than ever before. This renewed importance stems largely from the fact that in many cases, religions are distinctive, authoritative, and typically ultimate, modes of social identification and organization that involve "embodied practices," consisting in "networks of emotional connection" to transcendent goals or states. (Asad 1996, 1–15; 2005, 12) As such, there is no reason for the religions to be disqualified from serving to explain the world, since they are inherently part of the world of everyday life as much as politics or power. We just need to *reform* our notion of religion into a more usable comparative concept reflecting the many ways people the world over live in ways analogous to one another that can be called 'religious.'

Much of my thinking about the distinctiveness of religion, and thus the need for an equally distinctive term, 'religion,' arises in reaction to the events of 9/11. My intellectual strategy was to try to make sense of the hijacking events in a way that others had not brought to bear on 9/11. In the end, that strategic purpose of seeking to understand 9/11 led me to the identification of something that well deserved the name 'religion.' It further led me then to a definition of what this 'religion' in 9/11 was. Thus, as the Al Qaeda hijackers of 9/11 themselves demonstrated, and as Bruce Lincoln's recent analyses of them have shown, those agents acted on the basis of motives hard to classify as other than 'religious.' They behaved according to very different rules of what 'makes sense' than those we apply to calculations of 'costs and benefits,' typical of politics or economics. (Lincoln 2003) Their actions 'made sense' in terms of the powerful authoritative effect of their self-effacing *sacrificial* action – which, by definition, makes no 'sense' in economic or political terms. More properly described as martyrdom or sacrifice, arguably even more so than as jihad, suicide bombers confront us with a 'religious' way of 'making sense' – however gruesome or morally repellent such sense may be. (Strenski 2003a, 1–34) As Western, secular profit- and power-maximizers we were ill prepared to comprehend the extent to which the hijackers were agents of an authoritative social force that made its own kind of religio-political 'sense.' We simply had no clue that Al Qaeda 'sacrifice' (not suicide, as I shall argue) bombers were carrying out ritual and religious actions carrying a weight of traditional authority, as Lincoln has shown. (Lincoln 2003, 93–8) We simply failed to calculate the religious rationality of what they were trying to do, largely because we imagined that the things one might call 'religion' were just not important: religion was always *explicandum* but never *explicans*. Would it not, then, be sounder scientific practice to inquire whether religion is *explicans* or only as *explicandum* part of our theoretical research, and not its foreordained conclusion? In this book, I aim to 'put in a word for religion' by showing how 'religion' is an appropriate name for a factor *explaining* what happens in the so-called political world.

3

Interrogating 'Power'

'Power' is a notion which, while playing a central role in contemporary political science, is so obscure that it has scarcely justified this role. (Dumont 1979, 165)

1. Confronting the Paradox of 'Power'

In the previous chapter, I put 'religion' in the 'hot seat' of radical interrogation. There, I questioned the way we talk and think about religion, and in doing so I sought to get clear about how we might carry on talking and thinking about religion, less bedeviled by clichés. Now, 'power' needs to take its turn at radical interrogation. 'Power' needs to submit to a series of questions about the way we think with and about it, not least of all because we talk about power in a paradoxical way. On the one side, we talk about 'power' as forming a major bridge spanning the domains of both religion and politics. We often use the same word, 'power,' for both religious and political things. Accordingly, we talk of secular, material, or temporal 'power' in politics as easily as we speak of spiritual or eternal 'power' in religion. While it seems quite normal in politics to talk about the 'power' of 'power politics,' 'seizures of power,' 'power brokers,' or 'power-hungry politicians' and the like, our ordinary way of talking reflects that we feel it just as natural in religion to speak of the 'power of love,'

'God's saving power,' or the term 'holy power' that translates the Sanskrit term for the Ultimate, "Brāhman."

In fact, the way we commonly talk about 'power' also suggests much more than a *bridging* of two different domains, religion and politics. It suggests that we also think that the 'power' in religion and politics is the *same* power. Our common habits of speech — what I shall later indict as "bad habits" — lead us to talk of 'power' as such a unified field. Why else would we use the same term for realms of human life that, at least on the surface, seem so different? An unnamed preacher might say that

> Grace by the power of the Holy Spirit convicts us of our sins; and, oh, what power is needed to do that, to convince the natural man of sin! … What happens when you come to a proud Pharisee such as Saul of Tarsus? What can possibly convince and convict such a man of his sin? Again, there is only one power that can do it: it is the power of grace that can strike him down and make him cry, "Lord, what wilt thou have me to do?" (Acts 9:6)

But, is the 'power of the Holy Spirit' cited here the same as the 'fire power' of a 50 caliber machine gun? Is it the same any more so than the 'power' of 'power of purse' is really the same 'power' as that of the Roman Catholic priests to 'loose and bind' sinners? We speak of the American army being *power*ful because it smashed the army of Saddam Hussein, but we also speak of how *power*less they nonetheless were in the face of resistance to an occupying force. Is there are significant difference between a dominant 'power' *imposed* and an authoritative 'power' *accepted?* The French distinguish two words that we translate as 'power' — *puissance* and *pouvoir* — but the English seem satisfied with just the one — 'power.' Are Anglophones missing some key inner distinction as to the nature of 'power' that the French, for example, appreciate? While they may not rise to the level of clichés that I found with certain ideas about religion, when we speak about and with 'power' we speak commonly as if it were a single, unified domain of life. Accordingly, we do, after all, talk about the domains of secular, material, or temporal *'power'* alongside talk of religious, spiritual, or eternal *'power.'* We do talk about worldly or immanent 'powers' versus other-worldly or transcendent 'powers' and so on, as if they were things we could organize under the same rubric. Perhaps the word 'power' seems, then, as much at home in the realm of religion as it does in that of politics because our ordinary usage is telling us that we believe that 'power' is one thing.

Yet, despite our "bad habits" of speaking about 'power', we know deep down inside that the 'power' in politics of these examples differs from the 'power' in religion. The 'power' typical of politics is the power to force and coerce, typically by the use of violence. This 'power' is the ability to impose dominion in which the dominated need not cooperate other than to cease resistance to it. Indeed, the State, politics at its most typical, has been presumably well defined as that organ of society which monopolizes the use of force and that claims dominion. And, while I would not perpetuate the cliché, attacked in the previous chapter, that religion has nothing to do with power and coercion, monopolizing the use of force does not seem to *define* what is distinctive of religion. This may only be true of the conceptions of religion in the modern era, or outside such anguishing religio-political phenomena as suicide bombing in the Middle East. The Christian Middle Ages likewise differ as to their attitudes to coercive force, and so do suicide bombings in the Middle East. All I am saying is that in both cases, they claim that something more makes up their respective identities. Thus, if I had to specify a single thing that differentiates religion and politics it would be that, on balance, we recognize religion as working by way of 'power' in the sense of "authority" (*auctoritas*) even though it may employ force, while politics works essentially by way of monopolizing 'power' in the sense of dominion and raw coercive force (*potestas*), although authority, of course, matters to it as well. Indeed, sometimes *potestas* is constrained by *auctoritas* – sometimes the use of coercive force is blunted or is demoralized by a withdrawal of authority for its use. As R. S. Peters has argued, "'power' usually has meaning only by contrast with

64

'authority' rather than as a generic term of which 'authority' is just one species." (Peters 1958, 207–24, 220)

But while different, both the coercion, characteristic of politics, and the authority, typical of religion, are 'powers' in the sense that they are both ways of getting people to do what one wants them to do. Stalin did not challenge the pope's military 'power' in asking "how many divisions" he had. Stalin said this because he felt that the coercive force of armed might was no match for papal authority. Similarly, one imagines that the Chinese government appreciated the radical difference between these ways of getting people to do what one wants by showcasing brute power in the massacres of 1989 in Tiananmen Square. Similarly, it would seem darkly laughable to identify the cultural resistance grounded in the authority of the Dalai Lama with the 'power' of the coercive force dealt to Tibetan Buddhists by the People's Liberation Army – even if the Chinese fear the *auctoritas* wielded by the Dalai Lama. Nor is it irrelevant that military dominion – 'power' – over Iraq by American forces depends in some sense upon the authority of an otherwise reclusive and even quietist cleric like the Shi'a Imam Ali al-Sistani. Such examples, then, ought to make us reflect upon our gut feelings of discomfort in using the word 'power' to refer to the '*power* of love,' 'God's saving *power*,' or the term 'holy *power*' that translates the Sanskrit term for the Ultimate, "Brāhman." It is indeed paradoxical that we speak as we do about 'power.' And that in itself is reason enough to demand radical interrogation of it.

Thus, this fact of using 'power' to cover what seem to be different orders of reality raises the first item in the interrogation of 'power.' Why, despite our silent discomfort in doing so, do we talk as if 'power' were one kind of thing? *Should* we continue to talk and think of 'power' as naming a unified field? Given that there seems such a yawning gap between such oppositions as temporal and eternal, or material and spiritual, what makes us think we can avoid trouble using the word 'power' so broadly when we speak that way? That we talk this way indicates that we also think that we are talking about same kind of *power*. I concur with the epigraph of this chapter, from anthropologist Louis Dumont, that "'power' is a notion which, while playing a central role in contemporary political science, is so obscure that it has scarcely justified this role." (Dumont 1979, 165) For that reason, I shall argue in this chapter that we should be more aware that 'power' has a range of senses, and careful not to let our thinking fall into "bad habits" that may lead us into bad decisions. (Aron 1986, 253–77)

2. How 'Power' Plays Havoc with Thinking about "Institutional Violence"

An analogous example of one of our more egregious "bad habits" in talking about power comes in the way we often talk about violence in discourse about religion and politics as "institutional violence." I take exception to the use of this phrase, not because I think institutions cannot 'violate' human rights, such as the institution of Jim Crow laws, nor because I think institutions cannot act violently, such as a battalion of US Marines storming a beach, nor because 'violence' cannot be *institutionalized,* such as in our modern institution of warfare. I take exception to the phrase "institutional violence" because I think it fosters one of those "bad habits" of which Orwell wrote. It is a stealthy way of insinuating that there are only – at most – quantitative differences between acts of 'power' which involve physical force and those lacking it. Taken to its logical extreme, there would only then be – at most – a quantitative difference between, say, the 'power' involved in the "institutional violence" of a covenant that excludes me from owning a house in a given neighborhood and the violent power or force of being literally thrown out of my home, and so on. Yes, both cases are the same as members of a system of *injustice.* My point is that they differ as to violent power.

To be sure, in both the "institutional violence" of unjust property ownership laws and the violence of being removed from my home, the actuality of injustice is equally real. That is not the point in arguing for recognizing a certain difference – an 'edge.' What I do claim is that the locution "institutional violence" is a rhetorical device. It broadens the sense of the word 'violence' to cover a wide field in the same way that the word 'power' is used across a whole terrain of difference. Its purpose may well then be silently to authorize and condone – without explicit argument – the use of physical power or force – violence, proper – to overturn "institutional violence." There really would be, then, no *qualitative* difference between what is called "institutional violence" and physical power or violence. The two are regarded as just different forms of the same one thing, rather than categorically different. The strategic and tactical conclusion that follows, therefore, would be that it makes no difference as to how one opposes such so-called "institutional violence." Taking matters to their logical conclusion, were we to think about violence such that there were no qualitative difference between "institutional violence" and physical, violent power, we would be assuming that the use of physical violence in conflicts, say, over what one might call cases of "institutional violence" would not qualitatively affect the register and kind of those conflicts. Violence would have already been initiated by those perpetrating the injustice. The introduction of a certain level of 'power' would have already been made. On this view, both "institutional violence" and physical violence would be 'power' in the same sense: both forms of *violence,* and thus of the same kind. But, as a result, because a term like "institutional violence" collapses all things named 'violence' into one thing, the term 'violence' loses whatever logical edge it may have had over other kinds of conditions of injustice.

Now, I understand that this loss of logical 'edge' to the term 'violence' may well be more than sufficiently compensated for because "institutional violence" has an emotive 'edge' for those who wield it. I recognize the rhetorical force of a term like "institutional violence" for its utility in a struggle. But, aside from rhetoric, the use of 'violence' in "institutional violence" is, I would submit, really no different in meaning than 'injustice.' Using the term 'violence' adds a charge to discourse employing it, and thus aids the causes pursued in connection with it. If the term 'violence' means anything distinctive – if it has an 'edge' – its root meaning from Latin *"violare"* tells us that this term already denotes physical force. Thus, when Martin Luther King, Jr. and Gandhi warned against using 'violence' to remedy political and social injustice – what one might call cases of "institutional violence" – they were arguing against the use of *physical force*. When someone advocates the *violent* overthrow of the government – an overthrow necessarily involving the projection of physical force – they are advocating a materially coercive overthrow of a regime. The term "institutional violence" then builds on this primary meaning of violence by seeking to extend that meaning beyond the limits of the domain of literal violence to what one might call metaphorical or analogical violence. But the fact of such an extension should not be lost in the enthusiasm to embrace a potent metaphor capable of shaping how we think of power. Let me say why I shall not use the term 'violence' in the broad way embodied in such terms as "institutional violence."

Such considerations about our use of language make a difference to the extent that conflicts may change – often dramatically and qualitatively – when physical power such as violence – violence proper – is employed or is introduced. Even if both physical and metaphorical violence may weigh equally on the scales of *justice,* there seems a world of difference between metaphorical and physical ways of being violated. I say this in part out of the conviction that being an embodied material being matters in certain perhaps irrevocable ways. Being 'blind-sided' by an underhanded parliamentary maneuver in a faculty meeting and being 'blind-sided' in a football game differ – even if I might prefer taking honest knocks on the gridiron. Similarly, racial or gender discrimination may deprive me of life options, but – although it may be cold comfort – it does not necessarily *irrevocably* deprive me of my life. I suspect that this insight into the difference between violence and "institutional violence" lies at the heart of the thinking of Gandhi, Martin

Luther King, Jr., and, as we are witnessing today, the Dalai Lama. They not only believe – rightly or wrongly from a pragmatic point of view alone – that in 'violent' – physical – conflict they would be 'out-gunned' and not prevail. They also believe – rightly or wrongly – that once a conflict becomes violent proper – physically forceful, an act of real material power – it has a way of running amok into a kind of uncontrollable chaos that leads to endless uncontrollable recriminations, endless runaway attempts to even the score. It becomes our greatest human nightmare – a real 'war of all against all.' Violence itself seems to add another factor of its own to a conflict, beyond the substance of the conflict itself. But just imagine how a political campaign would change register were one candidate actually to 'kneecap' the other – precisely in the way IRA fighters often did to their enemies in Northern Ireland. Gandhi and King surely knew about struggle, and believed that 'real' violence was explosive; the Dalai Lama must know the same today. It was not just their loving-kindness that made non-violence their tactic of choice; it was a profound belief in the qualitative difference between violence proper and other non-violent forms of struggle and resistance that guided them – between violence proper and "institutional violence," if you will. If, then, one believes, as I do, that it makes sense to distinguish between physical uses of power and force – 'violence' as such – and those uses of power which are not, and therefore, which are non-violent, then it makes sense to reject the locution "institutional violence." Orwell again chimes in with the telling analogy and analysis:

> A man may take to drink because he feels himself to be a failure, and then fail all the more completely because he drinks. It is rather the same thing that is happening to the English language. It becomes ugly and inaccurate because our thoughts are foolish, but the slovenliness of our language makes it easier for us to have foolish thoughts. (Orwell 1956, 355–66, 355)

While the loose usage of terms like power has served a number of good ends, it has also confused our thinking about power and thus, about religion and politics. It has flattened discourse and prevented our being able to grasp the variety in human affairs. I am not engaged, therefore, in some kind of quibble about the uses of words. Significantly, this kind of subsumption of 'power' to 'politics' has blocked access to ways of seeing how religion has consequences in the political realm. This will be taken up in final chapter, where I shall bring together the results of the radical interrogations of religion, power, and politics to engage issues of religion and politics as they arise in the case of suicide bombings in the Middle East.

3. Whom Should We Blame? 'History' on Trial

Who, if anyone, is to blame for this way we think about violence, and thus, more fundamentally, about 'power' as if it were one thing? Answers to such questions of unexamined ordinary usage rarely, if ever, lie at the surface of things or in terms of the acts of individuals. Why does the Bible speak of God as male father-god, high in His 'high heavens,' rather than as female mother-goddess, profoundly anchored in the depths of Her earth – when we know neither is literally true? Why is it any more obvious why the numbers following 'ten' are 'eleven' and 'twelve,' rather than what logic might tell us that they should be – 'one-teen' and 'two-teen' – to match up logically with those that follow, 'thirteen', 'fourteen,' and so on? Answers to many of the questions about the 'way things are,' such as why we speak of 'power' as a unified field, are often historical questions. Things are 'this way' because of certain historical accidents, certain ways things just happened to turn out, even though they may well have turned out otherwise. I believe *part* of the answer why we find it natural to speak of power as a single thing is an historical question with an historical answer. What was it about the history of the West that has made it so easy – so 'natural' (sic) – for us to *think* and *speak* about 'power' as a unified field, as something including both spiritual and temporal under the same rubric? What, indeed, are the "conditions" in which all talk of the "ability to do something, to enact something, in connection with other persons, things, institutions" became talk of *'power'*? How did 'power' get its power, so to speak? How did 'power' achieve the hegemonic status it now (unthinkingly) has?

One intriguing answer to this query comes from structural anthropologist and Indologist Louis Dumont. In the latter part of his life, after a career writing on caste, kinship, and world renunciation in India, Dumont turned his attention to the historical and cultural origins of modern Western ideology. Treating our own culture now as the object of a kind of 'fieldwork,' Dumont focused his ethnographer's gaze onto the question of why 'power' occupied the privileged place in Western ways of constructing the world. Here, the anthropologist's practice of cross-cultural comparison paid dividends. When compared to us, the classical Indian system of social values expressed in the *varna* system did not privilege 'power' as we seem to do. Instead, the *varna* system ranked *dharma,* very loosely translated as 'morality,' 'moral or ritual duty,' and thus *authority* or something like *auctoritas,* over the social value of *artha,* again loosely translated as instrumental means, force, and thus 'power' or something like *potestas*. This ranking of values within the *varna* system corresponded, in turn, to a ranking of the social groupings seen as embodying these values – the brahmins or 'priests' embodying the *auctoritas* of *dharma,* over against the kshatriyas or military men, kings, and the like, embodying the *potestas* of *artha*. In the classical Indian case as described by Dumont, there is neither a privileging of power nor a conception of 'power' as a unified field. Why then do we in the West look at 'power' as we do, when at least one other great world civilization does not?

Comparison teaches us that things taken for granted as natural about ourselves need not have been so. Differences among societies result, in a way, from different 'choices,' deliberate and not, that they have made in the course of their histories. What we take for granted, for example, about 'power' might have been otherwise. Western society might have 'chosen' to be other than it is today, and 'history' would have taken different turns. What if the early republics of Italy had survived the onslaught of absolutism? What if figures like Gandhi, Martin Luther King, Jr., or Lech Wałęsa had been more prominent parts of our political history and not the latter-day entries – thanks in part to classic India – to it that they have been? Would a doctrine of divine right of kings have developed, and all that followed in reaction to it, had there not been already in place an equally absolute and competing theory of the divine right of popes – as secular rulers? Would there now be the system of nation-states in the West had the Reformation not occurred? (Philpott 2000, 206–45) These are all courses of history that might have been otherwise, given different kinds of choices made in the course of events. So how we become the kinds of people that we are is an historical question, and only history can provide answers to it. It was just this sort of realization of the contingency of the present that led Dumont back into the roots of Western civilization – into our classical past, into the history of the Latin West.

Now, when it comes to thinking about 'power,' any inquiry into its meaning leads necessarily back into Roman imperial history. If any institution stood for the embodiment of 'power' in ancient Rome it was the Empire. Its very name *'Imperium Romanum,'* called forth the principles of *'imperium'* and thus *potestas*. But, as well, in thinking about the Empire and power, we would need to think about other institutions that could have put imperial power into relief. Here, only the Church fulfills the requirement for such an institution significant enough to stand over against imperial power. Our everyday speech about 'power' – like our present-day refer-ences to God in *His high heaven* – has been determined by the structural, historical condition of major institutions. As the relation between major social institutions, like Empire and Church, changed, so also did our conventional ways of thinking and speaking about change – including, significantly, about the values that these institu-tions were felt to symbolize and embody, such as *potestas* and *auc-toritas*. Thus, if the relation between Empire and Church stood, in effect, for the opposition of *potestas* to *auctoritas,* then a change in the structural relation between these great overarching institutions would be felt, so to speak, at the level of individual attitudes and beliefs about those same values. Let us assume that in our society, the army, a force of 'might,' deposed the courts, a force of (legal) 'right,' and ruled in their stead. The logic of this argument suggests that at the level of everyday thinking, we would be constrained to draw the conclusion that the value of 'might' is triumphant over 'right.' Our thinking about the relation of right to might would be different than if, say, the army coup failed or was aborted.

A good place to begin in teasing out this relationship would be documented instances of struggle for supremacy between Empire and Church. How, in particular, might the resolution of these institutional struggles have shaped not only the relation between Empire and Church, but also our thinking about the values represented by each? How would it have shaped how we presume that 'power,' in the sense of political power, coercive force, etc., dominates the entire terrain of agency? How would we name the difference between the 'power' to confer sacraments, ordain priests, invest bishops, declare doctrine, and such proper to the church from the "'power of jurisdiction in the external forum'," that is to say, a "coercive power pertaining to a public authority … a truly governmental power"? (Oakley 2006, 79) What is implied about difference between Empire and Latin Church by the "unambiguous" refusal by Pope Gelasius I to grant the emperor "sacerdotal power," even while it was typically asserted by the Roman emperor in the East? (Oakley 2006, 77)

For Dumont, this opposition was best expressed as a distinction between two "entities or functions." (Dumont 1986a, 23–59, 46) The two "functions" or kinds of agency can be separated out as defining the agonistic distinction between the so-called "spiritual" over against the "temporal." (Dumont 1986a, 23–59, 50) Traditionally these agencies have been expressed as well in the opposition of the *auctoritas* of the priest over against the *potestas* of the king. (Dumont 1986a, 23–59, 46) In the early centuries a back and forth contestation afflicted those relationships. Especially in a time (third century) when the emperor presented himself as "an absolute monarch … above the law" – replacing the traditional title, *princeps* (king), with that of *dominus* (lord), and reducing "citizens" to "subjects" – a struggle to differentiate the empire from the Church would seem inevitable. The question persisted as to whom supremacy belonged. Which of these institutions was really superior – the Empire because it monopolized force and power (*potestas*), or the Church because it represented God's ultimate authority (*auctoritas*)? In consequence, which of the two different values, different kinds of agencies – *potestas* or *auctoritas,* was the higher?

The examples that might bring this conflict home are the clashes between the emperors and the Church over matters of religious doctrine, such as at the Council of Nicaea (325 CE). It "was inevitable," Dumont asserts, that at Nicaea Constantine would "collide occasionally with the claim of the Church to remain the superior institution." Acting in the role of the sacred king as he understood himself to be – even though still not entirely then a Christian – Constantine convened the Council at Nicaea. This act of convoking the council and ordering bishops to attend – all for the purpose of unifying the empire – neatly encapsulates how Constantine saw religion and politics as part of one thing. By contrast, the pope and Council "were keen on matters of maintaining" their *auctoritas* by "defining the doctrine as the basis for orthodox unity." Feeling all too well the threat to their *auctoritas* by the oppressive presence of the imperial *potestas,* the Church leadership "resented the rulers' intrusion in the preserve of ecclesiastical authority." (Dumont 1986a, 23–59, 45) In the East, St. Athanasius (373) stood as an early critic of "imperial interference in ecclesiastical affairs," while in the West, St. Hilary (367) did the same. (Oakley 2006, 77) "It is not true," therefore, as Francis Dvornik argues, "that the bishops were willing instruments in the hands of the imperial despots. This period of Church history is filled with hard struggles of the hierarchy for the exclusive right of defining Christian doctrine." (Dvornik 1951, 1–23, 22) Indeed, even though Christians generally accepted "ascribing a divine status to any ruler," and leading theologians tried as well to shore up intellectual support for such a view, in the West, resistance to sacral kingship persisted. In the West, Empire and Church, thus, stood in uneasy, unresolved conflict with one another as representing two different sets of interests and two kinds of reality. This constant fishing in the waters of the other rendered the relation of Empire and Church intellectually incoherent. (Oakley 2006, 77) That neither Empire nor Church had a satisfactory way of thinking about each other blocked any possible practical resolution to their conflict.

But, in about 500 CE, something of a theoretical resolution of this uneasy relation between Empire and Church was attempted by Pope Gelasius I (492–6 CE). In his letter of 494 to Emperor Anastasius, the pope promulgated what Steven Ozment has called "perhaps the most balanced statement of the relationship between secular and ecclesiastical power." (Ozment 1980, 139) This expressed a theory that sought at least to address the conflict between Empire and Church, *potestas* and *auctoritas,* at the level of theology and thought – even if this left practical conflicts to be resolved in their own terms. While the emperor could no longer be conceived as having "any sacerdotal office," neither could the clergy aspire to governmental office, by their own right. Addressing the emperor, Gelasius wrote of this new understanding:

> Two there are … by which this world is chiefly ruled, the sacred authority [*auctoritas*] of the priesthood and the royal power [*potestas*]. Of these the responsibility of the priests is more weighty in so far as they will answer for the kings of men themselves at the judgment. Know … that, although you [Emperor Anastasius] take precedence over all mankind in dignity, nevertheless you must piously bow the neck to those who have charge of divine affairs and seek from them the means of your salvation … For if the bishops … recognizing that the imperial office was conferred on you by divine disposition, obey your laws so far as the sphere of public order is concerned … With what zeal ought you to obey those who have been charged with the administration of the sacred mysteries? (Tierney 1964, 13–4, quoted in Ozment 1980, 139 n. 8)

In effect, Gelasius viewed the two conflicted "entities or functions" – the priest's *auctoritas* and the king's *potestas* – as related in terms of a rather subtle mutuality. Instead of opposed autonomous agencies placed into polar opposites, they were brought into an intimate legal relationship with one another. Some sort of essential balance and reciprocity was achieved, if only in theory. Instead of submission of kings to priests, or priests to kings, Gelasius posited an interrelation defined by an essential give-and-take, an institutionalized interdependence. The Church and Empire were thus not externally cobbled together in some makeshift arrangement. In Gelasius' words, the "priest is subordinate to the king in mundane matters that regard the public order," so by the very same token, the "king is subordinate to the priest in spiritual matters." (Dumont 1986a, 23–59, 46) As subjects of the Empire, the priests fall under the rule of the imperial government, but the then widely accepted "notion of emperor's priesthood" – however ill-defined – is dismissed: "'the emperor no longer assumed the title of priest, nor did the priest claim the royal dignity.'" (Oakley 2006, 77)

This relation of institutions dictated, in its turn, a corresponding actual relationship of the exercise of complementary 'powers' – *potestas* and *auctoritas*. The *potestas* of the king, therefore, requires the submission of priest and his *auctoritas* in temporal matters, while the *auctoritas* of the priest demands submission of the kings' *potestas* in spiritual matters. This is just the opposite of saying that kings wield spiritual *auctoritas* or that priests now have temporal *potestas*. It is to say that each recognizes the prerogatives of the other in their own proper domains. (Oakley 2006, 78) The two agencies live off of each other, without becoming each other. They are not separable independent substances, since they are both needed to make up the social whole. (Dvornik 1951, 1–23, 20)

The same complementarity can be detected in classic India's relationship between brahmin and king. Classic Indian society is thus not a contracted assemblage of independent substances, brought together out of convenience to deal socially with one another. They are parts of an organic whole – different levels of a single structure. Thus, they 'belong' to each other by being necessary parts of the same totality. Thus, while brahmins may flatter themselves as "religiously or absolutely superior to the king," they are not superior in any absolute sense – and certainly not in kingly matters. It is of the very nature of a brahmin that they are "materially subject" to the Indian king, and thus that they 'belong' to him as he does to them in ritual or religious matters. (Dumont 1986a, 23–59, 46ff.) Likewise, when we return to Gelasius, we must interpret this pope's attempt at reconciling *potestas* and *auctoritas* as putting them into a hierarchical relationship of complementarity that the ancient Indians would well understand. Thus, "if the Church is in the Empire with respect to worldly matters, the Empire is in the Church regarding things divine." (Dumont 1986a, 23–59, 48) There simply is no Roman social world for Gelasius unless these two agencies 'belong' to one another essentially. How far can authority in a political context go without power as *potestas?* Not far at all, Gelasius seems to say. Can the 'powers that be' rule without the legitimating, supporting 'power' of authority? Not much at all, Gelasius, again, seems to assume. As political philosopher Joseph Raz has pointed out, "the right to rule" is complemented by the "obligation to obey." (Raz 1986, 23) And, further, when society survives, it is "in part because at least some of the subjects accept" the claim of rulers to rule. (Raz 1986, 27)

Gelasius' delicate, arguably unsustainable, ideological balancing act was not, however, to survive for much more than two centuries – even as a piece of theory. The two agencies of *potestas* and *auctoritas* were to become ever more confused. Even as early as the fifth century, for example, the Church began to assume "public functions" in Rome, such as for health, education, and welfare. (Oakley 2006, 94) When confused in this way, *potestas,* in effect, edges into the domain of *auctoritas,* and in practice, overwhelms *auctoritas,* in effect, by compromising its independence. 'Power' proper – *potestas* – tends to reduce all other agency to itself, *auctoritas* included. Thus, from as early as the fifth century, the Church became a "compulsory, all-inclusive, and coercive society, comparable to what we call the state and, in its totality, well-nigh indistinguishable from it." (Oakley 2006, 94)

Things may have passed a tipping point of the Church's establishing itself as the "real State of the Middle Ages in the modern sense" with the fateful anointing of Pepin the Short as King of the Franks by Pope Stephen II in 754 CE. (Figgis 1998, 15) The Church would recognize the legitimacy of the Carolingian line, and bless it in a special way by administering kingship through a holy unction. The Franks, for their part, defended the Church's interests, and in Italy endowed the pope with a vast area of the center of the peninsula under his perpetual temporal government and dominion (*potestas*). In 800 CE, the papal coronation, and anointing, of Charlemagne as Emperor of the Romans further established his bona fides as a kind of sacral king with serious religious responsibilities for his subjects. (Oakley 2006, 98) We should thus not neglect the manner in which the Franks reintroduced sacral kingship onto the scene, nor the way Charlemagne, in particular, saw himself as a "Christian ruler" responsible for leading his "Christian people" toward salvation. But, at the same time, not only did the pope crown and anoint Charlemagne, thus blessing the Carolingian line as the beginning of the Holy Roman Empire, but from that time, culminating in the era of "papal monarchy" from the eleventh through fourteenth centuries, the popes themselves became "supreme political" authorities as well. As J. Neville Figgis tells us, "The Holy Roman Empire ... did attempt to realize the idea of an all-powerful State, but that State was the Church." (Figgis 1998, 14) This situation would last through the Middle Ages, such that with the papal "claim to an inherent right to political power, a change is introduced in the relation of the divine to the earthly: the divine now claims to rule the world through the Church, and the Church becomes inworldly in a sense it was not heretofore." (Dumont 1986a, 23–59, 50) Both Church and emperor claimed to rule by virtue of their *potestas*. We thus think about power as a unified field rather than as an arena of complementary difference because the Church simply ceased representing the spiritual alone. It took on a temporal role, while the emperor added or augmented a spiritual agency to his manifest temporal profile. Put otherwise, at some identifiable historical point, the spiritual became temporal and the temporal became spiritual. At some point, what had been two distinct principles – the spiritual and the temporal – had ceased being distinct, but instead became two forms of the same thing – 'power.' As the distinction between Empire and Church shrank, the popes assumed the role of the emperors in the West, and the principles of spiritual and temporal collapsed into one another. What *auctoritas* they claimed derived its strength from their political power. We now live with the results of these historical processes by thinking about 'power' as we do.

Despite his attempts to bring both agencies under common submission to the common interests of the social whole of which they formed constituent parts, Gelasius' delicate contrivance was undone. One might say that both the agencies representing once solely *potestas* or *auctoritas,* respectively, went their own ways – with *potestas* assuming the principal place. Thus, in place of "Gelasius' hierarchical dyarchy," by the tenth century CE the Church became the basis of a fully fledged "monarchy of unprecedented type, a spiritual monarchy." Thus, in the West, despite Constantinian and Frankish attempts to realize a "sacral kingship" like that of the Eastern Empire, we get rather the "kingly priesthood" of the Roman Church in the West. (Dumont 1986a, 23–59, 50) The efforts of the so-called Gregorian reforms of the eleventh century insured that kings would no longer be able to claim sacrality, nor that they could continue to "invest" bishops with "spiritual symbols of ring and pastoral staff." The pope would claim jurisdictional superiority over the emperor, and he, not even God, would claim to be the real power source behind papal unction. (Oakley 2006, 112) Over against Gelasius' dyarchic system where the Church was in the Empire, but the Empire also in the Church, the Gregorian reforms put the Empire squarely *in* the Church. This meant, as Pope Gregory VII wrote in a letter to Bishop Hermann of Metz (March 1081), that the "'priests of Christ are to be considered as fathers and masters of kings and princes.'" (Oakley 2006, 115) The popes would, in effect, deny sacrality, or rule by divine right, to the emperors, but claim it for themselves. This made them the "true ... successors to the erst-while Roman emperors." (Oakley 2006, 116)

The ultimate lesson for us here in this interrogation of 'power' is that it matters little who held the scepter of dominion, because in the case of either the Church or the 'State,' the political – 'power' proper – gains the upper hand. Henceforth, the spiritual and temporal realms are unified at the expense of the spiritual. The ultimate moral of this tale for us is that both emperor and pope, along with the agencies of their reign, are referred to as "powers." The term 'power' proper – *potestas* – now also names *auctoritas,* since it too is now just a 'power.'

This historically specific confusion of the agencies of *potestas* and *auctoritas* explains a host of other apparent anomalies in the world of religion and politics. Why, for example, does an otherwise worldly institution, defined by its monopolization of the use of force, violence – 'power' in the sense of *potestas,* the "modern State" or nation-state, assume a religious character? Why does it become, for example, the focus of absolute obedience, for which individual citizens not only *do* sacrifice their lives, but also feel that they are *obliged* so to do? Why does the nation-state as well assume the monopoly of the use of *potestas* – force and violence? Why is its authority – *auctoritas* – over life and death virtually unquestioned? Why does it assume other functions of *auctoritas* – namely the right to demand obedience, the right to rule, and the duty to be obeyed? (Raz 1986, 23–6) Why else is it considered the natural focus of the highest personal and communal loyalties? After all, other large collectivities do not make such demands, even though the modern corporation seeks to make them. Why does it, in this way, become a "bearer of absolute values" – transcendent spiritual elements – that one would normally assign to God, or another such religious entity?

The collapse of Gelasius' contrivance suggests an answer. That the nation-state should possess such remarkable qualities shows, therefore, that it "is not in continuity with other political forms," such as the Frankish migratory band, the Roman *patria, civitatas,* or

Greek *polis*. It "is a transformed *Church*." (Dumont 1986a, 23–59, 51; my emphasis) From this lofty position as a "transformed Church," the modern State and its values of *potestas* hold sway universally and, thus, have their authority. As a "transformed Church," the modern State makes absolute demands for sacrifice, for absolute loyalty, for recognition of its transcendent claims to allegiance – for authority that once belonged properly to the Church as its main distinguishing feature. It is a 'power' – indeed *the* power as well as font of all power, the hegemon monopolizing the use of force. As such, the modern State also lays claim in practice, at least, to the highest authority – *auctoritas* – in the human world, despite the occasional protestations of some religious folk. Here then is the uplifting secret of the anachronistic 'speaking truth to power,' the edifying secret of those distinctly unfashionable movements of resistance to *potestas* by an *auctoritas* wielded by a Martin Luther King, Jr., a Gandhi, or a Dalai Lama. Here, on the other hand, is the less edifying secret of why we think about power in a way which plays into the hands of the "transformed Church" – why we think about injustice as mediated by physical force or violence, proper – why we reduce injustice to "institutional violence." Here, as well, is why we think about all manner of agency as modes of the power proper to the hegemon of force, the "transformed Church" – power proper – *potestas*.

4. History's Helper: We Should Also Blame Foucault

But our remote history is not the only cause of why we think of power as a unified field, proper to politics. History has had some helpers, notably Michel Foucault. His present popularity has had a lot to do, I suggest, with the renewed life won by our ethnocentric prejudices about 'power.' It is from Foucault that we get talk of power as "the general distribution of energy within a social system." (Chidester 1988, 7) Foucault has given rise, then, to looking at power as a "pervasive dynamism or tension existing in a particular network of social relations … a complex network of forces, tensions and energy that constitute a political system …" Rather than being focused on the State, "power is a dynamic energy that infuses a social system." (Chidester 1988, 8)

What is owing to Foucault in this discourse about 'power' cannot easily be put in a few words, but surely his location of subtle and multipolar sources of domination, and the need to resist and struggle, must take the lead. Foremost is Foucault's original reprise of the idea that 'knowledge is power.' Foucault thus refers to his work here as seeking to incite an "insurrection of knowledges" that will expose how our ways of conceiving the world enable certain regimes of power. If knowledge is power, then Foucault wants to expose the many hidden ways it has been so to the detriment of human liberation. Disciplines touting their 'scientific' credentials often form the objects of Foucault's skillful undermining of their claims of freedom from such calculations about power. For Foucault, that they are regimes of knowledge is sufficient to implicate them in regimes of power. It is "really against the effects of a discourse that is considered to be scientific that the genealogy must wage its struggle," says Foucault. For Foucault, that regimes of knowledge classify and categorize things gives them tremendous power, because it is in terms of those classifications that we act toward those very things. (Foucault 1980, 84)

Foucault's major effort is decidedly liberationist. He seeks something of a transformation of our politics. He wants to "imagine new schemes of politicization … which will take new forms" in order to facilitate liberation – in particular, liberation from "the vast new techniques of power correlated with multinational economies and bureaucratic states." (Foucault 1977b, 183–93, 190) Accordingly, Foucault's theoretically rich and culturally suggestive historical writings have spawned a generation of thinking about how individuals and institutions control others by the most subtle, obscure, and unintentional methods. Because of the broad scope of Foucault's subject matter – human sexuality, systems of classification, asylums and prisons – it is easy to see how his work could speak across disciplinary lines in the university. Think only about the unintended way in which our pervasive Enlightenment humanism preached liberty and reform, but how its institutions, such as the asylum, often enacted regimes of the harshest forms of dehumanizing domination. These dehumanizing processes got their start from the 'enlightened' *knowledges* that rigorously categorized and classified human beings and their behavior and gave the dehumanizers *power* over other human beings.

While we owe the great French historian and philosopher many things, Foucault's approach to 'power' actually reinforces our own cultural historically formed prejudices about 'power' that I have exposed in the previous pages. In this way, despite his reputation for revolutionizing our thinking, Foucault actually reinforces all the deeply entrenched prejudices that have been historically built up in the Western way of thinking about 'power.' It is probably enough that in making 'power' the major theme of his entire intellectual oeuvre, Foucault has reinforced our 'native' (sic) tendencies to prefer the conflict model of human sociability.

But there is more. In Foucault, we find no separation of *auctoritas* and *potestas*. Power is unitary and it is political. Paradoxically, while Foucault says that he seeks to think about power outside the 'real world' of *everyday* politics of the State, he nonetheless produces a concept of power that is purely political. For him, the "set of relations of force in a society constitutes the domain of the political." A "politics is a … strategy for co-ordinating and directing these relations." Bringing 'power' back in, it then follows, *a fortiori,* for Foucault, that

> Every relation of force implies at each moment a relation of power … and every power relation makes a reference, as its effect, but also as its condition of possibility, to a political field of which it forms a part. To say that 'everything is political' is to affirm this ubiquity of relations of force and their immanence in a political field … (Foucault 1977b, 183–93, 189)

And, there is still more. Foucault's determination to see power only as the political further results in Foucault's seeing power within human institutions as war. For Foucault, then, war is a quintessential political act and thus the soul of power. Says Foucault,

> None of the political struggles, the conflicts waged over power, with power, for power, the alterations in the relation of forces, the favouring of certain tendencies, the reinforcements, etc., that come about within this civil peace – that none of these phenomena in a political system should be interpreted except as a continuation of war. (Foucault 1980, 90–1)

Foucault here stands, then, for a frank and unapologetic declaration of an extreme form of the conflict model as the basic story line of the human past and condition. (Foucault 1980, 90; Taylor 1985a, 152–84, 170) All the ordinary associations with extreme forms of the exercise of power, such as warfare, conflict, and struggle (and not, significantly, the more neutral term, 'agency'), form the stuff of history and always will do so. Putting it directly, having 'power' in Foucault's sense is to construe human relations in strictly political terms, in terms of conflict, coercion, domination, and the other norms of political behavior in our world. It entails that every use of 'power' is seen as being political – and, in a sense, even that takes into consideration Foucault's point that human life in general is seen as involving plays of power at every step. The commonplace claim that the 'personal is the political' is a salient symptom of this kind of thinking. (Minogue 1995, 5–6) Thus, in the humanities, talk of politics is ubiquitous. Power – and power proper as *potestas* – is ubiquitous. It owns the field of play in large part because of the prestige of Foucault.

5. Problematizing Power in South Africa

So, what happens when we put together Foucault's notion of power with religion? In a crude version of this relation, we can see Foucault's fixation on power in the writings of a contemporary figure in the study of religion:

Religions thus become the most finely tuned examples of power structures, patterns of force which control human lives and dictate how they are to be conducted. Make no mistake about it: religions are about power, about the power to be given you and about the power which controls you. (Lease 1994, 453–79, 474)

The same writer then links power with politics in a way Foucault would find amenable. For this writer, the consequences for under-standing religion are clear. In forming the idea of 'religion,' power is subsumed to politics. "'Religion' is a key node for the distribu-tion of power or control over … consciousness. Religion, in other words, is ultimately and always a political manifestation, and a theory of 'religion' must always also be a political theory." (Lease 1994, 453–79, 459) But such statements leave us disadvantaged at the level of abstract theory. What might Foucault and his theory of power look like 'on the ground,' when religion is involved?

Historian of religion in South Africa, David Chidester, provides something of a taste of how Foucault looks 'on the ground' in southern Africa at least. Let's begin with the way Foucault's convic-tion that 'knowledge is power' takes shape under Chidester's direc-tion. Referring to anthropologist Louis Leakey, Chidester notes how Leakey categorized the Mau Mau as a 'religion' where once he had classified them as a "political" group. Leakey thus alters our 'knowledge' of the Kikuyu, in the same sense as Foucault might say that classifying certain inmates of eighteenth-century asylums having this or that mental 'illness' would. Some consequences regarding power then must flow, according to Foucault's theory. What are they?

Interestingly, this reorientation of 'knowledge' about the Kikuyu occurred at the same time that the Kenyan colonial government was also exerting its power – its coercive force (*potestas*) – literally to confine thousands of Kikuyus during the Mau Mau rebellion – under recommendations as well coming from Leakey. Not surpris-ingly, Chidester is drawn to this coincidence, and offers a typically Foucaultian reaction to it. The shift in 'knowledge' of the Kikuyu corresponds to a shift in their relation to the 'power' of coercive force. And, more or less in line with Foucaultian orthodoxy, Chidester sees Leakey's exertion of classificatory agency as equivalent to the imposition of hardcore coercive force – of political power in the sense of *potestas*. Thus, Chidester says,

> In the midst of a war zone …, Louis Leakey tried to reinforce a colonial conceptual *closure* around the Mau Mau movement by *designating* it as a religion. This *conceptual containment* coincided with the *literal containment* of tens of thousands of Kikuyu in prisons and "rehabilitation" camps. (Chidester 1996, 256; my emphases)

While I have not the slightest intention of defending Leakey or the colonial Kenyan administration, we might try to penetrate behind Chidester's figures of speech in order to try to understand what Chidester is really claiming here.

I find Chidester's conclusion tortured, unpersuasive, and frankly absurd. If Chidester is saying anything, it is that Leakey's reclassification – his "conceptual closure" – played a role in *causing* the physically coercive – "literal containment" – of Kikuyus. He cannot simply be making the charming point that the two kinds of 'closure' and 'containment' make for a nice sort of literary resonance. As Chidester says, with my emphasis: "Leakey tried to reinforce a colonial *conceptual closure around*" flesh-and-blood people. Surely, then, against Foucault's theory, this exposes the fact that 'knowledge is *not* power' in the sense of coercive force, or *potestas?* Chidester makes the mistake of running together actually putting people '*under* arrest' with thinking about them '*under* a certain rubric.' Granted our 'knowledge,' our classification of the Kikuyus, will facilitate the exercise of certain kinds of 'power' against them. Labeling someone an 'enemy combatant' in a military conflict will bring sure results in whether or not they are thought to be a fair target for extermination. But, while one thing may lead to another, the two things are simply not the same things. Knowledge may be power, but power is not really unitary!

Chidester could have been a lot more precise had he said that setting the Kikuyu 'apart' under this category or the other logically *reminded* him of setting people 'apart' into prisons, or was metaphorically like doing so. But to call these metaphors by their right names would, I believe, present problems for Chidester. Different sorts of senses of 'power' would have to be admitted and a strict form of Foucaultian orthodoxy about power as unified field would not be able to stand. Instead, Chidester makes the seemingly unwarranted claim that Leakey counseled the colonial government to 'contain' the Kikuyu, *because* he had classified parts of their culture in a certain way as religious. What evidence do we have from Leakey, or any one else for that matter, to elide his urging of physical 'containment' with his 'containing' of Kikuyu culture within the boundaries of one concept of religion rather than another – especially when that new designation is as a 'religion'? And, even if conceptual 'containment' could be shown to cause or condition physical 'containment,' would not any concept applied to the Kikuyu presumably do so, and not just 'religion'? Yes, like thousands of other white settlers in Mau Mau Kenya, there is every reason to believe Chidester when he says that Leakey was eager to see perceived enemies safely secured. But that desire of Leakey's is just local 'politics,' indeed the essence of politics – 'power' as *potestas.*

If my desire to mark proper distinctions about kinds of 'power' was only to make a point of logic, I might be guilty of merely quibbling with Chidester's work. In actuality, this turns out to be far from the case. Because Chidester buys Foucault's reduction of all forms of 'power' to one, and to one that is essentially that of *potestas,* he blinds himself to the reality of different agencies. He winds up treating all exercises of power as if they were one, and in doing so treats real criminals as little different than those who are not. Specifically, Chidester lets perhaps the leading academic promoter of State-sponsored and administered apartheid policies – himself an actual official agent at the heart of the South African apartheid policy – virtually off the hook of responsibility for the exercise of real coercive force. W. F. Eiselen receives a bare page and half of generalities about his role in the execution of real 'confinement' of Africans when, as we have seen, Chidester goes on and on about Leakey's metaphorical 'confinement' of rebel Kikuyus under the rubric of 'religion'! (Chidester 1996, 252–3) Blame for such a misdirection of attention rests perhaps less with Chidester than with Foucault, whom Chidester aims to emulate. As I shall argue in the next chapter, as Michael Walzer argued before me, Foucault's obsession with power and politics ironically "desensitizes his readers to the importance of politics" in the sense of State politics and its exercise of coercive force. (Walzer 1986, 51–68, 66) Foucault has misled Chidester and caused him to let go scot free the real 'bad guy' in charge of exerting real power over African folk by subtly manipulating how they were classified!

My purposes here are not mainly to skewer David Chidester's work for its own sake, but to use it as "Exhibit A" in an interrogation of power as it has come to be conceived and put into play with religion. It shows how ideological and moral fervor in the study of religion and politics, inspired by Foucault, may too much dominate what we do. It shows how we need to interrogate this construction of power as much as some have relished interrogating 'religion.'

6. Foucault versus Foucault

The first step in doing this fundamental groundwork on 'power' is to achieve some degree of liberation from the powerful hold Foucault's thought has on us. In this way, we can see its 'edges,' so to speak. And, in this way, we can 'see round' it to what I believe are some deeper perspectives on 'power' and 'politics,' and thus on religion and politics. But of Foucault can one not ask whether one might em*power* oneself – learn to paint, dance, swim, and so on – without domination of others creeping in? And, is speaking of power in such contexts really the same as talking about power in those others, where competition and struggle against an opponent are the norm? Even the language of competing or struggling 'against oneself' ought to be suspect as overextending an analogy and masking a different sort of agency of its own. Does not such talk tell us more about our unreflective determination to insist upon a unitary politicized notion of power and agency than it may about the actual nature of the range of agencies and enablements that come into play? Are acts of enablement – either self-referential or shared with others – for example, learning to sing, alone or in chorus, learning to dance, alone or with others, necessarily best described as exercises in *power,* or are they equally well regarded as enrichments, enhancements, enablements, and so on, rather than war? Neither painting nor dance is a martial art. Can we not sing, dance, or paint as well without being 'political' in any meaningful sense? Are we really at 'war' when we enable ourselves by taking up water colors? Of course not. But that is what Foucault would have us believe, and what a too close alliance between his thought and the new liberationism means. We must reject this way of thinking as too narrow to be helpful in understanding human beings. We need to 'see round the edges' of Foucault's narrow perspective if we want to make progress in thinking about religion and politics.

Oddly enough, the person who may best help us think round the edges of the Foucault we have met thus far is his worthy successor, the Foucault of his last years. In some of his last writings, especially in the second and third volumes of the *History of Sexuality,* Foucault seems to adopt a perspective that at least allows for the possibilities I have opened up. (Foucault 1988, 16–49, 35) There, he brings out the ancient Greek practice, the "care of the self," or the "progressive consideration" or "mastery" of "self" brought under the rubric of Stoic askesis. But as if to turn his earlier self on his head, Foucault sees this taking care for oneself not as "political activity" at all. (Foucault 1988, 16–49, 26) Indeed, Foucault as much as recants the Foucault put to use by Chidester, even if he cannot quite let go of the ill-fitting language of "domination." There in his 1982 lecture, "Technologies of the Self", he says:

> Perhaps I've insisted too much on the technology of domination and power. I am more and more interested in the interaction between oneself and others and in the technologies of individual domination, the history of how an individual acts upon himself, in the technology of self. (Foucault 1988, 16–49, 19)

Better late, than never, I suppose.

7. Thinking about Power as *Auctoritas* and Hierarchy

If this chapter's interrogation of 'power' proves persuasive, what then should follow about the focal concern of this book, religion and politics? If I am right that our thinking about 'power' has been one-dimensional, why not improve it by at least making it two-dimensional? Because of historical reasons peculiar to the West, we have slipped into the routine of thinking about 'power' in only *one* way – as unified political force, coercion, violence, and such – as *potestas*. But, if so, then our interrogation shows that we might resist historical determinism by also thinking about 'power' as *auctoritas* as well. If we can sort out these two senses of power, we would also be well placed to explore religion and 'power' in more than just the single dimension of 'power' as *potestas*.

I should like to conclude this chapter, then, by bringing out this other dimension of 'power' known as authority or *auctoritas*. This other dimension of 'power' merits being called 'religious,' as I have suggested in Chapter 2, particularly when our theoretical strategy is one of understanding the interplay of what we might call religion and politics. That is to say that while both *potestas* and *auctoritas* can be found in all sorts of social formations, whether these be politics, religion, the arts, and so on, I am offering what I believe to be a fruitful way to distinguish a religious aspect in otherwise purely political contexts by following a particular distinction between *potestas* and *auctoritas*. In many cases, of course, there will be *no reason* to distinguish a *religious* dimension to otherwise purely political events. But deciding whether we should pick out a *religious* aspect will depend upon our larger intellectual or polemical purposes and strategies. I believe the present situation of human bombings in the Middle East may be one of those situations in which it would be useful to separate out something reasonably called a 'religious' aspect – as I shall argue in the final chapter.

Thus, I refer again to the formula stated earlier of how we might define 'religion' in such a strategic context of distinguishing religion and politics. This yields the following formula: while a given 'religion' may display both *potestas* and *auctoritas,* 'religion' is inconceivable without *auctoritas,* but conceivable in the absence of *potestas*. But, on the other hand, while politics too may reveal a mixture of both *potestas* and *auctoritas,* it is conceivable without *auctoritas,* but not without *potestas*. In the concluding chapter, I shall discuss how we can better understand the relations of religion and 'power' by appealing to the example of human bombings in the Middle East. From my point of view, human bombings can usefully be said to be political acts, since they project power in the form of coercive force – *potestas*. But I urge that it would be particularly valuable to understand them in their being 'religious' acts, projections of power as authority – *auctoritas* – made meaningful, moreover, in part by their drawing upon Islamic traditions. Seeing 'power' as a differentiated, rather than as a typically *unified,* field, gives us greater insight into how things happen in the world.

Thus, far from laying down some absolute distinction between religion and politics, I see them merging in their coordination of both senses of 'power.' The human bombings in the Middle East actually merge religion and politics, even if it is useful to tease apart the ways in which these two dimensions of human life act. It is by understanding this 'merging' of different kinds of 'power' that I believe we can make sense of a phenomenon like human bombings in the Middle East. This is why I shall argue that such bombings – whether we like them or not – ought to be understood as both 'potent' secular *jihadi* attacks and 'authoritative' religious sacrifices. They present cases in which the fundamental conventional wisdom about religion that I have called clichés is exposed for what it is in its crudest forms.

Without anticipating my conclusion, I might only point out the obvious – that if one can argue successfully that the human bombers represent a religious phenomenon, marrying *potestas* to *auctoritas* – both sheer political power and religious authority – then several conclusions follow. One of them would topple the cliché that religion is always good, since – depending upon one's point of view in the struggle – there is as much reason to judge human bombing *bad* as it may be good. The invocation of Islamic authority for such actions does not make such human bombing 'good' any more that just pointing out its obvious political aspects would necessarily determine that it was 'bad.' And that is only one cliché about religion and politics that falls to the wayside when we scratch below the surface of our thinking about religion, power, and politics.

But meanwhile, let me draw the pertinent conclusions from the discussion of this chapter. This entire chapter has been pointing inexorably toward an interrogation of power that demands a full discussion of the concept of *auctoritas*. We know how and why we have come to think about 'power' as we do. What, then, are we to make of 'power' in the sense of authority, *auctoritas?* What is *auctoritas* that it should be separated out from power as most often understood – namely as *potestas?*

R. S. Peters claims that understanding *auctoritas* is the "key" to understanding 'authority.' Besides providing an etymological understanding of our word 'authority' from its Latin source, *"auctoritas,"* understanding *auctoritas* as the Romans did also gives us a deeper understanding of authority itself. Understanding *auctoritas* is thus the key for our understanding more deeply the complex meaning of 'power.' Understanding *auctoritas* helps us better grasp the distinction between power as *auctoritas* (authority) and power as *potestas* (force). And understanding that distinction helps us see more deeply into the parallel distinction between Church and Empire, and thus religion and politics. So, a good deal more is at stake in exploring the meaning of *auctoritas* than an academic question about the meaning of a Latin word. Our basic concepts of religion, power, and politics all get their meanings from ancient sources whose influence carries on to this very day in shaping the way we think about those things. We begin with *auctoritas*.

For the Romans, *auctoritas* was originally a term referring to the solidity of a legal contract or to the worthiness of the testimony of a witness. Later, the reference of the term shifted to the "respect or dignity or weight attached" to the witness or document and such. By extension, someone who added this "dignity or weight" to a transaction or document came to be called an *auctor,* since they, in effect, gave greater value to or created permanence and the like to whatever was said to possess *auctoritas.* The Latin word *"auctor"* carries with it both senses of the English word 'author,' since an *auctor* can be both a writer and someone who acts creatively. (Friedman 1990, 56–91, 74) It is, however, the sense of *auctor* as creator that lives on longest in the formation of our ideas of authority. It is the *auctor* as the source of "producing, invention, or cause" which "can be exercised in the spheres of opinion, counsel, command and so on" that lives on longest among us. In this sense, in matters concerning *auctoritas* or authority, the author, *auctor,* is essential. Thus, in "social life, whether we like it or not, there are such auctores." They "are producers or originators of orders, pronouncements, decisions and so on." It is through them that "social regulation is brought about." (Peters 1958, 207–24, 210) R. B. Friedman is of the opinion, therefore, that William Gladstone's definition of authority best captures the focal place of the *auctor* as 'adding' to what was there before. Says Gladstone:

> The proper idea (of "auctor") is that of one who adds. In strictness, this must be adding to what existed before, as a witness adds to the thing his testimony about the thing ... the use of the word author for writer is strictly correct, and belongs to the original sense.

Part of what *auctores* add is their mediation of things at one level to those at another level:

> An "author" comes between us and the facts or ideas, and adds to them a ... ground of belief, in his own assurance to us respecting them ... And hence perhaps we obtain the largest and clearest idea of "authority," as that which comes between us and an object, and in relation to us adds something to the object which is extrinsic to it ... (Friedman 1990, 56–91, 75; Gladstone 1877, 3–4)

In effect, then, implicit in the notion of *auctoritas* – authority – is *hierarchy*, because the existence of 'levels' or gradations comes immediately into play. The *auctor* mediates between levels of reality by adding things to one level from another, or from him or herself. This is typically what heroes and savior-gods do the world over. Saviors 'bring' salvation; heroes 'give' us hope. But in neither case can they thus be our *equals* – because it is upon their mediation that we depend – even as the success of their mediation itself depends upon our *acceptance* and *recognition* of it. Neither saviors nor heroes act in a vacuum; they certainly cannot succeed in a vacuum. Interdependence is essential to the success of their roles. Thus, the *auctor's* mediation needs to be accepted, or recognized, by those for whom they 'add' something. It cannot be coerced, as is the natural way for *potestas* to act. Gladstone, then, saw both the author and authority as sharing the common property of being part of a system of dependence. It is the authority or author upon whom one relies. Someone else's judgment is thus placed ahead of one's own. (Friedman 1990, 56–91, 76)

Since a system of authority is necessarily a system of inequality, it places one in a state of obligation toward the one in authority – the *auctor*. Authority entails a debt of duty toward the *auctor*. Authority is in part the ability to compel obedience; it is the way we get others "to do what we wish." (Friedman 1990, 56–91, 59) Consequently, in times or places where the values of individualism and equality reign, our obligations will tend to irritate us, and the hierarchies they presume will seem burdensome. Authority will then naturally also come under suspicion, as the bumper-sticker slogan of the rebellious 1960s said 'loud and clear': "Question Authority!" This may be one of the reasons that we 'moderns' have suppressed authority. We'd just rather not face our need for it. We resent it because it sets a disagreeable 'bit' into our mouths. Indeed, when the principles of individualism and equality reign, the assertion of the importance of authority will, at best, be given careful scrutiny, at worst, be judged harshly and, perhaps, peremptorily. Hierarchy simply does not fit in with our conventional individualist–egalitarian way of looking at the world.

This overall sense of unease with authority among us modern individualists makes it relatively easy for us to suspect that those in power often enough exploit people's trust in authority. We are on alert to the possible readiness of those in power to mask their readiness to enforce their authority by using coercive force. Historian of religion Bruce Lincoln will thus go so far as to claim that force and violence are "implicit in authority." Authority "may deploy force," supposedly at any time and for whatever reason. We must be particularly vigilant, then, about authority, since it thus "harbors a capacity for repressive violence" that "liberal defenders" of the distinction between authority and coercion seek to maintain. In a way, Lincoln's view is a kind of materialist mirror-image of Weber's notion of the mysterious "charismatic" force at the basis of authority. On Weber's view, the reason people submit to authority is not because they see vaguely behind the veil of 'legitimate' authority the hard-nosed face of coercion lurking there, but because the person or institution in authority has a special magical power Weber calls "charisma." (Eisenstadt 1968, 21ff.) Both Lincoln and Weber, then, in their different ways, resist treating authority on its own terms, but instead seek to ground it in something else entirely. Wise counsel, then, for those seeking to retain authority, ultimately based on either force or charisma, respectively, would be to resist pushing their authority too hard, lest they dislodge the "fig leaf" hiding the "naked force" or lest they expose authority as kind of magic trick of illusion. (Lincoln 1994, 6)

Whether or not Lincoln's attempt to collapse the notion of authority into coercion – *auctoritas* into *potestas* – can be sustained by the actual practice of authority, the hierarchical nature of authority remains. The only problem with Lincoln's virtual reduction of authority to coercion is his simultaneous desire to say that authority depends upon "trust" (Lincoln 1994, 8) or "commonly shared" opinions. (Lincoln 1994, 10) No matter, however much Max Weber invokes the pure magic of charisma in authority, Weber, too, tells us how important the "recognition" of charismatic authority is to its power. Weber is telling us how important so-called 'intangibles' like 'trust' matter in human affairs, and thus how other factors besides power count for us. (Eisenstadt 1968, 20) What both these examples show is that, while people can be subtly cowed into submission, for example, by brute force masquerading as authority, as Lincoln suggests, there is a point at which all authority depends upon *acceptance* of that authority. All authority presumes hierarchy – something we egalitarians don't particularly like admitting. Likewise, Weber knows how effective the "threat of force" can be, but he also knows that this is always a "last resort." (Eisenstadt 1968, 16) Short of these extreme cases, what remains in the normal exercise of authority is the requirement that authority be "legitimate," that it be "accepted," that people willingly subordinate themselves to each other. R. S. Peters, for example, claims that,

> ... the term "authority" is necessary for describing those situations where conformity is brought about without recourse to force, bribes, incentives or propaganda and without a lot of argument and discussion, as in moral situations ... (Peters 1958, 207–24, 218)

Peters is telling us, in effect, that the power of authority needs then to be traced as much to properties of the *auctor* – either as 'one who adds' or as a kind of magician – as to the community that 'accepts' the *auctor* as an authority. It is only under conditions of interdependence, mutuality, reciprocity – hierarchy – that authority 'happens.'

Now, when such a notion as the power deriving from communities arises, the person whose name naturally comes to mind is the French sociologist Émile Durkheim. It is from Durkheim that we can learn the most about the how society can be said to exert 'power' that is at once not brute coercion, nor the force of a good argument.

8. What More Is to Be Done? Thinking about Power as *Auctoritas* and Social Force

Beyond *auctoritas* involving a non-coercive kind of power that works by way of mutuality, recognition, acceptance, and hierarchy, *auctor* means something like the Durkheimian ideas of the negative and positive social factors shaping human action. These are what Durkheim referred to as social "constraints" and "forces," respectively. As to negative social factors – the "constraints" – for Durkheim, their "paradigm sense" was "the exercise of authority, backed by sanctions, to get individuals to conform to rules." Here is the *auctoritas* of social control – the 'power' of the collective opinion, social pressure, moral obligation, duty, that which must be obeyed and such. On the positive side, for Durkheim, social "forces" were also inspiring "causal factors inducing men" among other things to "break the rules." (Lukes 1972, 13) Here is 'authority' as more than duty. Here is the authorized act that Durkheim saw as "desirable." In Durkheim's sense, both "goodness and duty" are part of every obligation. "A certain desirability," said Durkheim, is "no less essential than duty." (Giddens 1986, 155)

In its positive, desirable aspect, *auctoritas* gives people the confidence to innovate and exert themselves creatively – parallel to the Durkheimian 'sacred' that is also "good, loved and sought after." (Giddens 1986, 155) This 'empowerment' has virtually nothing to do with the negative conception of the constraining relation of religion that we saw articulated at the beginning of this chapter by Gary Lease, such that religion is about "patterns of force which control human lives and dictate how they are to be conducted."

(Lease 1994, 453–79, 474) Nor is this 'empowerment' anything like Foucault's talk of "political struggles, the conflicts waged over power, with power, for power" that "should be interpreted except as a continuation of war." (Foucault 1980, 90–1) This is not, then, 'power' as *potestas*. Rather, this is 'power' as *auctoritas* – what the Durkheimians called "dynamogenic forces." It is to reprise Gladstone's notion that the *auctor* is the person who 'adds something to' our common life. Here be heroes! Here are they who 'add something' to common life by mediating levels of reality.

These creative energies characterize moments of "collective effervescence," when new ideals and beliefs are born. (Lukes 1972, 13; Pickering 1984, 209–15) What is more, Durkheim identifies the site in which these "dynamogenic forces" are actualized and released as religion. Even more than this for the Durkheimians, "the principal function of religion is dynamogenic." Religion as an agent of the 'power' of *auctoritas,* in effect, "produces social energy – it must be seen in the mode of activity and change." (Pickering 1984, 214) Thus, when Louis Dumont complained that "'power' is a notion which, while playing a central role in contemporary political science, is so obscure that it has scarcely justified this role," (Dumont 1979, 165) he meant to issue a warning. He was challenging the Leases and Foucaults among us about their assumption that power was either only a negative constraint or the imperialistic *potestas* of political 'power.' While it is that in part, it is also *auctoritas*. Our problem – induced as it has been by the history of the West – is that we have come to think about power as one seamless field, rather than as a domain of complementary difference. What had once been two distinctly distinguished principles – the spiritual and the temporal, corresponding to *auctoritas* and *potestas* – became two forms of the same thing – 'power.' When the distinction between Empire and Church dissolved, and the popes assumed the role of the emperors in the West, our Western way of thinking about 'power' changed too. But we do not have to live with this way of thinking. We can expand our notions of 'power' to embrace a greater sense of authority – *auctoritas*.

in political affairs," or even the more precise "methods and tactics involved in managing a state or government." The best that can be said for such definitions is that they at least delimit the everyday and commonsense meaning of these words. But, when we seek to go deeper, we find, along with Carl Schmitt, that as with 'religion' and 'power' one "seldom finds a clear definition of the political." (Schmitt 2005a, 20) Nonetheless, we can recall some of the distinctions we made in earlier chapters about the projection or exercise of power, namely the exercise of *potestas* and *auctoritas* – power in the sense of coercive force and authority. For the most part, the usage of 'politics' has involved the management of some sort of collective body, no matter whether that be a Greek city-state, the *umma* or khalifate of Islam, a collectivity ruled by Louis XIV or an Indian *rājā,* the Han, British, or Roman Empire, the Roman Catholic Church of the Middle Ages, or a modern nation-state.

But what makes an inquiry into 'politics' even more interesting is neither the minimal sorts of definitions we find in dictionaries nor the qualitative differences we find between kinds of despotic political regimes and modern politics, but two further points. First is the question of how the 'political,' considered as a domain of life, is related to other domains of human behavior. Is the political, as "political realists" would say, a more or less distinctive, even *autonomous* domain of human life, especially with respect to morality and religion? Or, while retaining some distinctiveness, does it overlap with other parts of the human world? Does it make any sense, for example, to speak of *both* political *and* religious *auctoritas* or authority as proper to these notions? And, if we would go so far as to speak of an autonomous 'politics,' how is such a claim to be justified?

Second, while there is considerable consensus that the political necessarily involves affairs of state, is this perhaps, as Michel Foucault has argued, too *narrow* a designation? Would it be better to pursue an intellectual strategy that regarded 'politics' as something that pervades all parts of the human condition insofar as we seek to enhance our own power? Would it perhaps better serve the purpose of resisting the tendency to separate out the political from everyday human affairs by embracing a definition that states 'everything is political'? Would it fulfill a more plausible theoretical purpose to define 'politics' so broadly as to encompass the struggle for domination, power over others, power for ourselves, and so on, under one rubric? I believe that answering these two questions requires recognizing that 'politics' is a constructed, but limited, concept that is deeply ironic.

2. Where There Is No Politics: Despotism and Totalitarianism

The first step in any attempt to get historical purchase on the category of politics is to upset its universal, essential, or trans-historical pretensions. As it happens, the modern English words having to do with politics show an intense historicity and embeddedness in a series of projects. Tim Fitzgerald claims that the "meaning of 'politics' is not historically constant; it does not run essentially unchanged from Aristotle up to the present." In fact, Fitzgerald does not believe that the word 'politics' is used in the modern sense before the later seventeenth century. (Fitzgerald 2007, 150) Instead, we get the evolution of related usages, ending in the 'political' emerging in reified form. Thus, we move from the attribute "politic" – signaling "suitable and appropriate" action – into the "politic body" – signaling a proper or "well-ordered" commonwealth. (Fitzgerald 2007, 154, 155) Modern as well is our word for that strange beast, the 'politician.' The word does not appear until 1586 in George Whetson's *The English Myrror*. The original French word *'politicien'* is not much older. This murky historical provenance of the modern term 'politics' may be one reason to sympathize with political philosopher Carl Schmitt's lament that one "seldom finds a clear definition of the political." (Schmitt 2005a, 20)

This historicity of the term 'politics' may account for some political thinkers, like Kenneth Minogue, saying that in traditional despotisms or in modern totalitarianism, *politics* does not exist. More precisely, the institutional bases of the term 'politics' do not exist. Institutions proper to politics, like citizenship, constitutions, parliaments, and assemblies, "the state as an abstraction" – none of these exist. (Fitzgerald 2007, 19; Minogue 1995, 3; Skinner 1978, 352–3) At court, or in the king's household, there will surely be gossip galore, vendettas without end, and all sorts of maneuvering within a circle of elites. There is, moreover, behavior that is judged 'politic.' But, there is really no politics, because there is no territorial State or 'body politic' apart from the very physical body of the monarch. There are only quarrels and associations that congeal about the concrete, physical person of the monarch. The so-called international 'politics' of pre-modern monarchies scarcely differ from the feuds of Mafia 'families' like those played out on television between the rival DeMeio and Lupertazzi crime 'families' of *The Sopranos* fame. Quentin Skinner claims that it was not until the 1576 publication of Jean Bodin's *The Six Books of the Commonwealth* that "the state as an abstraction" is "separated from the person of the sovereign." (Fitzgerald 2007, 19; Skinner 1978, 352–3) Either way, this radical reduction of the meaning of 'politics' in the pre-modern West signals absence from the 'public square.' Politics is supposed to happen only inside the private, personal, or domestic life of the monarch. Like the king's garments, or the affairs of his personal household, politics in the sense practiced by despots is really none of anyone else's business – and intended precisely so to be. How much, by contrast, were the procreative acts and child-bearing events of monarchs the public business of the realm. Subjects had a spectator's interest in the gender of an heir, the consummation of a union, or the health of a dynasty, but a despotic monarch pursued a policy in which he or she was the only 'player' in the 'game.' Not so for us: politics is not only *is* everyone's business, it *should be* everyone's business. Politics is a citizen's *duty* and, for some, the acme of public life. When Robespierre memorably argued for the formal execution of Louis XVI, he declared that the king "must die because the nation must live." (Walzer 1992, 134) Robespierre – as well as the regicides of the English Civil War – thus gave gruesome voice to the insight that politics as the private affair of a king, whose very body is the 'body politic,' and whose head was once bathed in the anointing oil of monarchy, comes to an end *only* when that monarch is ritually unanointed – when that anointed 'body politic' is dismembered and dissolved – when that governing head is ritually and solemnly severed from its compliant body. This is no less than to say that traditional despotism, focused as it is on the person of the prince, represents a politics that is no politics at all.

Similarly, in modern totalitarianism, the domain in which politics happens is effectively reduced by design to the inner workings of the inner party. Although modern totalitarianisms are quintessential "power states," they deliberately have no politics, or at best, a politics so curtailed as to be reserved for the few, in order to serve the strategic interests of those 'few.' Raymond Aron pointed out this paradox of totalitarianism by noting that on "the other side of the Iron Curtain, Power (*Pouvoir*)[*potestas*] is terrifying because it encompasses the whole collectivity and is reserved to a minority." (Aron 1986, 253–77, 276) Similarly, we might want to turn a critical eye upon ourselves and the easy cynicism and impatience that frame so much of our sneering public talk about politics and politicians. We should not smugly think that the appetite for an end to politics fed only the rise of the totalitarianisms of the past. It is a dish always ready to be warmed up and served anew.

Ironically, religion, in the eyes of many, is as quintessentially 'private' a matter as was the politics of the pre-modern or totalitarian Western despotisms. In its familiar construction, religion has vacated the 'public square' to take refuge in the inner sanctum of the human heart and personal conscience. Religion is little more than a matter of having certain beliefs, of enjoying certain inner experiences, that is to say, in effect, of being the perfect mirror image of the secular or 'political' realm as modernity comprehends them.

3. Autonomous Politics

But what makes the concept of 'politics' even more interesting is at least another point of an ontological sort. Neither politics as construed by the minimal sorts of definitions we find in dictionaries, nor the categorical differences we find between kinds of despotic or totalitarian regimes, fully bring out the radical nature of our historically constructed assumptions about the political. Here, thanks to Machiavelli, Hobbes, and others, politics, like 'the free market,' is imagined to be an autonomous, independent realm of human life. Speaking of this process as the "Great Separation," Columbia's Mark Lilla argues that the West achieved "the liberation, isolation, and clarification of distinctively political questions, apart from speculations about the divine nexus." For Lilla, this meant that politics "became, intellectually speaking, its own realm deserving independent investigation …" (Lilla 2008, 162) Prominent proponents of such an autonomous politics are those called "political realists." Case in point is their doyen, the political philosopher Hans J. Morgenthau, and his better known latter-day disciple, Henry Kissinger. For Morgenthau, the political is "autonomous" in the sense that he defines politics as having no *'history,'* since it is something absolute and timeless: "Politics, like society in general," says Morgenthau, "is governed by objective laws that have their roots in human nature." Further, the "laws of politics … have not changed since the classical philosophies of China, India, and Greece endeavored to discover" them. (Morgenthau 1965, 4) Of other sources of value in the 'public square' – law, morality, religion, etc. – one "cannot but subordinate these other standards to those of politics," says Morgenthau. (Morgenthau 1965, 11)

One should not imagine that Morgenthau defined 'politics' as the autonomous master of human life out of 'thin air,' in the abstract. Morgenthau's definition of 'politics' was tailor-made to fit the intellectual purposes and policy strategies that he thought his world required. As a refugee from Nazi Germany, writing and thinking in the midst of World War II, he lived in an ominously threatening world. More than that, he had already become convinced by his devotion to Nietzsche that the moral values of the West were in a state of dissolution. (Frei 2001, ch. 5) This left only politics "as the determining force shaping reality within and between nations." (Frei 2001, 143) Thus, for 'realists' like Morgenthau, in such times, and more generally perhaps, it is the political that reserves the right to regulate economic life, and to demand the allegiance of religious or moral communities. The conviction that politics is such a unique and independent sphere of human life is, on its other side, to assert its claim to freedom from things we call 'economic' constraints, or 'religious' and 'moral' reservations. It is to assert, as well, the right and duty of the forces seeking to preserve human values, such as the Allies of World War II, to make politics their sole guide. The rise of Hitler had proven to Morgenthau and other 'realists' that political idealism was a weak and useless philosophy in a time when only hard 'realism' could prevail against enemies of great intensity. Woodrow Wilson, perhaps the most notable exponent of the "moralist-legalism" school of political idealism opposed by Morgenthau, said that a nation "is great, also, very great, in its moral force." (Wilson 1913) But a political realist of the Morgenathau camp like George Kennan was quick and sharp to attack Wilsonian idealism: "A nation which excuses its own failures by the sacred untouchableness of its own habits can excuse itself to complete disaster." (Kennan 1952, 73) Such a perspective gave definite shape to Morgenthau's definition of 'politics' in realist terms.

It is thus we, in the history of the West, who have given birth to this politics and its strange and singular offspring, the 'politician' or, better yet, the '*professional* politician.' As the great Max Weber argued, this being enters politics not as a mere "avocation" – as some *casual* or "'occasional'" pastime, but as a member of a freshly emergent species of human being. Politics is thus a "profession" – nigh unto a sacred 'calling' – a "vocation." (Weber 1946, 77–128, 83)

This creature thus may both live "for'" politics – as an avocation – or "'off'" politics – as a profession or career. (Weber 1946, 77–128, 84) As a "'leading politician'" or "minister," this creature "*consciously*" cultivates policies as a kind of "art." (Weber 1946, 77–128, 89) Yet, in the West, Weber contends, this new creature is not to be confused with that figure found everywhere – the person who serves and counsels the prince. While this creation of ours may do politics in the dedicated "service" of some lord, Weber argues that it is only in the West that the professional politician serves powers other than the prince in a dedicated and routinized, professional, way – as a "professional" politician. (Weber 1946, 77–128, 83–4) In order to serve such powers other than the person of the prince, one requires, as we will see, the emergence of 'politics' or the political domain – as we have seen, "the state as an abstraction ..., separated from the person of the sovereign." (Fitzgerald 2007, 19; Skinner 1978, 352–3) There are no 'politicians' outside the larger strategies of social transformation which makes their existence possible. Again, politicians do not fall from the sky, they do not occur in the abstract, but in the course of the flow of historical purposes and events.

4. Where Our 'Politics' Makes No Sense

Besides looking into our own history in this way, we can get purchase on the cultural singularity of our notion of 'politics' by submitting it to the chastening rigors of cross-cultural comparison. Two prominent admirers of the British anthropologist E. E. Evans-Pritchard – Mary Douglas and Louis Dumont – have called attention to Evans-Pritchard's refusal to grant our notion of 'politics' universal, abstract application or autonomous status. Douglas doubts, for example, whether the Nuer folk of East Africa "can be said to have anything corresponding to political institutions." (Douglas 1980, 62) At best, the "Nuer political scene is sparse, practically empty," she adds. (Douglas 1980, 64) And there "is no accumulation of power. The phrase 'ordered anarchy' seems to describe the situation." To assume that the Nuer had such a politics, would, according to Mary Douglas, as it would for Asad with 'religion,' amount to a "careless imposing of ideas from one culture to another …" (Douglas 1980, 63)

For Dumont's part, he too doubts the universality of politics as a cross-cultural term: citing Evans-Pritchard, Dumont notes that "there is no guarantee that, just because modern societies clearly distinguish the political dimension, it makes a good comparative dimension." (Dumont 1975, 328–42, 337) Like our assumption of the universality of the 'free market,' the "political approach fits into … [our] habit of thought, while other approaches would challenge its validity." (Dumont 1975, 328–42, 338) In conceiving politics as autonomous and universal, we thus may well be engaged in a devious exercise of protecting an investment in our own precious categories and our own precious plans. Worse, however, than just protecting an entrenched way of thinking about the world, recent history teaches that presuming the autonomy of politics – say from religion – in international affairs can lead a country into costly policy missteps – such as in the Muslim world. There, as we are slowly – perhaps – learning, religion and politics are not automatically separated out and considered autonomous of one another.

Thanks, then, to the efforts of anthropologists like Evans-Pritchard, it becomes highly problematic whether we can assume the universality of an autonomous "politics." Yes, the Nuer ally themselves to others or alternately quarrel with them; they fight and feud, individually and collectively; they mediate their fights and feuds, alliances and treaties. But the Nuer do not separate out such activity as 'political.' "Organized political life" simply does not exist among the Nuer. (Evans-Pritchard 1940, 181) Thus, whatever else we find among the Nuer, we do not find an emergent politics or autonomous political system. There will then be no Nuer Machiavelli, no Nuer Hobbes nor Hans Morgenthau nor Henry Kissinger.

5. Politics, the Construct

'Interrogation' is based on the assumption that, to a significant degree, at least in the modern West, politics is a constructed category, like the 'economy' understood as an unregulated market. How, then, have we constructed ourselves into the 'political' or 'economic' animals that we are – even to the extent of repressing how and why we have done so? What I mean by this can perhaps better be grasped by considering the emergence of the economy.

In his classic of economic history, *The Great Transformation,* Karl Polanyi tried to explain how the social norm of a 'free market' came to be dominant in our society – how the emergence of the category of the 'economic' as an *autonomous* feature of life happened. (Dumont 1979, 164 n. 75a) How was it that behavior indicative of the presence of market values seems to have pervaded the whole of our society? How is it that these market values are not just confined to ordinary commodities, but have tainted human relations? How is it that human relations, and in a sense, humans themselves – even excluding slavery – have become commodified, have come to be treated as things?

Polanyi argued that the long, slow, but nonetheless, deep social and cultural transformations of Western history put economic or market values into a particularly vexing relation to the rest of human life. (Polanyi 1944) Polanyi shows how, over a course of centuries, markets and market thinking – economic rationalization, profit maximizing, valuing things over persons, and so on – went from being "embedded" within society to embedding society in the market. Polanyi shows that historically the values typical of markets had been at one time subordinated to overarching social values, such as relationships based on affection or familial loyalties, prerogatives of the ruler, local custom, and such. Later, however, economic life, understood as market economy, came to be seen as something that should not be regulated, that was best left to be free and autonomous.

We can track Polanyi's claims historically by the record of restrictions laid upon market activity by institutions such as the political structure or the Church. Here, everything was jealously regulated to suit the needs of the political and religious structures of society. They insisted upon everything from the hours and days in which markets could function, to the regulation of import and export, to the setting of prices and wages, to the 'guild' system of regulating entry into and practice of trades, to the exclusion of land and labor from the market economy, to 'blue laws,' and so on. But as crucial items became commodified, notably as land, and as trade barriers fell, the balance tipped against the political and religious structures, and the markets no longer were really capable of being regulated. The economy became in this sense autonomous and free. Market power had, in a way, overwhelmed the forces traditionally restraining its reach and grasp, and thus broken free of constraints to its activities. Everything and anything were 'for sale' – legitimate items for exchange within a market. Society, in the end, has come to depend on markets in a way not so before. Society was, as Polanyi put it, "embedded" in the market. And this includes our politics too, insofar as economic values constrain political choices.

A further point in raising this example of the emergent autonomy of markets and economic values is to offer that we live in a world in which certain values have become so deeply ingrained that we think of them as 'natural.' We feel that this is the way things have always been and will always be. But, thanks to Polanyi's historical research, we know how things had indeed been otherwise with the so-called economic parts of our lives. 'Free' markets are neither natural, nor are they the primitive condition of essential humanity. This observation, in turn, enables us to imagine how things might be otherwise in the future. We can, therefore, at least free our minds from the dominance of our present-day contingent state of affairs, and do what we can to change, or at least, try to maneuver around the restraints created by historical processes as best we can. For the purposes of this book's argument, this means that, as Polanyi has interrogated 'economy' or 'market economy,' so also we can interrogate 'politics.' We can, in this way, become skeptics of the way people want us to believe that things really are when they invoke the word 'politics.' In doing so, we can take the first steps toward freedom from this sort of conventional wisdom, and begin to conceive the world in newer ways.

As for politics, an analogous transformation with analogous results also took place in the history of the West. There had been no (autonomous) politics, yet one came into existence. Politics, in this sense, *emerged,* and along with it the discourse and rhetoric of 'politics.' Thus, there have been, and are, everyday experiences that we commonly call 'political,' such as struggles for power and influence, matters of sovereignty and other forms of collective combat, decisions about who is to rule and by what means, and so on. Today, we could also cite examples of politics such as marching in protest demonstrations, fasting for peace, running for elected office, being outmaneuvered in a departmental meeting, working for the election of a local city council member, trying to understand the motivations of invading armies and resistance forces, characterizing why young men and women become suicide bombers in the Middle East, and so on. All these things that we readily label under the heading 'politics' are things that I have 'seen.' But I have never *seen* an autonomous thing called politics as such. That is because there are no data for politics as an autonomous reality, anymore than there is some 'thing' we could indicate as 'religion,' 'art,' 'the free market,' and so on. The word 'politics' is a term we use to organize kinds of behavior, kinds of primary data, under a rubric that we believe names a unique and essentially autonomous reality. 'Politics' is a 'construct' that we create to advance certain purposes and strategies. 'Politics' is a name we apply – consciously or not – for interpreting certain data that we wish to single out as belonging to a common class of things in the world. That is why there are literally "no *data* for 'politics.'" It is we who assign the name 'politics' to certain classes of data.

6. Two Pernicious Views of 'Politics'

Let me begin my confrontation with conventional ways of imagining politics by taking on this belief that our word 'politics' names an *autonomous* entity. I reject the view that 'politics' names such an underlying substratum, free of the *historical* process and from 'contamination' by other such 'things' in our world – 'art,' 'morality,' 'the market,' 'religion,' and the purposes or strategies we attach to them. I thus take issue, then, with the great economist, and father of the school of Political Realism, Hans Morgenthau. In his "Six Principles of Political Realism," Morgenthau affirms, right off the bat, that the political is "autonomous." Says Morgenthau, "Intellectually, the political realist maintains the autonomy of the political sphere, as the economist, the lawyer, the moralist maintain theirs." (Morgenthau 1965, 11) Indeed, but, as I have suggested all along in this book, in the *abstract, none* of these deserves the autonomy they claim, even if we can usefully speak of their distinctiveness relative to certain theoretical purposes and strategies. To be fair to Morgenthau, while he does not deny that these other 'things' – law, morality, religion, and so on – may be factors in considering human affairs, "he cannot but subordinate these other standards to those of politics." (Morgenthau 1965, 12) Morgenthau's assertion of the autonomy of politics naturally entails that that politics has no *history*. "Politics, like society in general, is governed by objective laws that have their roots in human nature." These "laws" have "not changed since the classical philosophies of China, India, and Greece endeavored to discover these laws." (Morgenthau 1965, 4) This means that politics is a single, natural, and cross-cultural 'given' feature of a universal and unchanging human nature. There is, and always has been, one and only one way of being political, in the same sense that free marketers believe that 'free – autonomous – markets' have always existed, and that people have always been exclusively market-driven in any transactions that one might call economic. We, as human beings, are, and have been, not only 'profit maximizers' by nature, but power (*potestas*) maximizers at the same time.

The second assumption about politics I wish to confront is the obverse of the first. This view asserts that politics is not some sort of self-contained, autonomous domain, such as Morgenthau might entertain, but instead is a kind of all-pervasive human quality. Instead of saying that politics is a specially delimited, autonomous domain of life, everything now becomes political in the same degree. The view that *everything* is political is best exemplified by Michel Foucault. Recalling what was discussed in the previous chapter, let me remind readers of what Foucault said on this matter:

> Every relation of force implies at each moment a relation of power ... and every power relation makes a reference, as its effect, but also as its condition of possibility, to a political field of which it forms a part. To say that 'everything is political' is to affirm this ubiquity of relations of force and their immanence in a political field ... (Foucault 1977, 183–93, 189)

It might also be noted that in both views, the 'conflict model' reigns supreme. Whether one is making special claims for the distinctiveness of an autonomous politics, or whether one is painting the whole of human life with the same brush, both views see human life as fundamentally an arena of conflict, not cooperation, contest, not conviviality, suspicion, not trust, selfishness, not cooperation, self-assertion, not common values. We are not by nature social, and therefore, cooperative beings, but somehow autonomous individuals that need to be coerced into life together. We are not made for friendship, but for enmity.

I shall argue against both the Morgenthaus and the Foucaults that their beliefs about 'politics' are especially damaging for understanding human life. We thus need to overcome these assumptions because they prevent us from having fresh and informative ideas about such human matters as the relation of religion and politics. These are views that, in their own ways, are as unexamined as the six clichés about religion that I attacked in Chapter 2. Like all clichés, they impoverish our thinking, and thus hamper our attempts to understand ourselves, including those things we call 'religion' and 'politics.'

Over against these two items of conventional wisdom, I shall argue two points. First, I shall develop an analysis of the genesis of our politics in historical and culturally specific events of the history of the West. Unlike Morgenthau, I argue that politics as we know it has been historically conditioned. Moreover, what we call 'politics' has often been identified with what we call 'religion' in particular, or indeed, has been generated by this religion, so-called. At one time or place, 'we' had nothing worthy of the name 'politics,' but rather a conglomeration of differently named factors and institutions. But, at another time and place, 'we' came to have such a 'thing' as a politics. This history charts a certain distinctive feature of our own culture, namely the specific conditions of the rise and persistence of the nation-state, or State, and in particular, its relation to being a "transformed Church."

I am thus committed to the view that our history might have turned out other than it has. We might have neither 'religion' nor 'politics' nor 'art' and so on. What, for example, if Pope Gelasius' formula of mutuality between Empire and Church had held? What if the popes and emperors had not abandoned their mutual respect and forbearance with respect to one another and the different agencies – *auctoritas* and *potestas* – they represented? What if the State, as a "transformed Church," could not claim absolute monopoly over the use of force – *potestas* – but, unlike an institution that considered itself the autonomous embodiment of *potestas,* had to negotiate its use of force with other organs of society? What if the State, thus, lacked the benefit of being such a "transformed Church," with all that means in terms of enhanced *auctoritas* derived from the sense of the nation-state as a sacred being? What if boundaries between 'nations' were, thus, not sacrosanct, and their trespass not the reason for armed conflict or mass deportation of 'illegal' immigrants or 'alien' elements? What if the State did not need to be the unified thing we imagine that it does, such that a confusion of ethnic or religious groups within its borders did not represent some kind of contaminating trespass requiring radical purging? What if it were not 'mortally sinful' for the nation-state to permit 'states within the State,' such that local autonomy and variety within the State were matters for the celebration of difference and diversity, not preludes to pogroms or massacres? Such considerations cause me to be skeptical that our present institutions and classifications are somehow 'natural' and inevitable. In this chapter, I see politics as an historically contingent reality, and one whose genesis I intend to interrogate.

Second, I shall confront the related idea, much bandied about, that everything is political. Where this claim is not straightforwardly "vacuous," it harbors a questionable belief about the nature of social life. As to the emptiness of the claim, Tim Fitzgerald states that "struggling for power," for example, is "so endemic in the struggle for survival that using the word 'politics' to describe so many different potential contexts of power renders it descriptively and analytically useless." (Fitzgerald 2007, 169) As for a general view of human life that sees politics everywhere, this view represents itself as a realistic view of human life, but reveals instead a cynicism that distorts our understanding of how and why people act. It is to impose a conflict model onto human relations that overlooks the vast areas of human life where conflict is irrelevant. I am also thus arguing that 'politics' does not exhaust the domain of what we call 'public.' There is far more to life in public than politics, even though politics is a vital part of public life. In this sense, Leon Wieseltier's observation about the contingency of our thinking in categories, such as 'politics' or the 'political,' bears recalling:

> The confidence of the political philosopher is mocked … by the unruliness of human affairs. For, before the philosopher comes to circumscribe the reach of economic behavior, or to judge the claims of religion upon social life, people are already buying and believing, selling and unbelieving. They have not waited for the philosopher to put their thoughts and their actions in order, nor have they lived all their inner and outer lives with a view of their political implications. (Wieseltier 1991, 80–99, 80)

115

These two points come together in an especially troubling and powerful way when we start to think conjointly about religion and politics. There, politics seems to me at its most salient when the role of the State gets its due, rather than when we imagine politics to be some general and diffused aspect of the human condition. It is just such a notion of politics as related to the emergence of the State or nation-state that I shall try to defend as especially germane to some of the biggest issues in religion and politics today – especially matters of religious violence. The paradoxical effect, therefore, of saying that 'everything is political' is to blind oneself to some of the more anguishing ways that politics and religion engage each other in our world today. That engagement will occupy us in the final chapter's discussion of so-called suicide bombings in the Middle East as a test case for the new thinking about religion and politics I have tried to encourage in this book.

7. History Lessons for Professor Morgenthau

Our politics is not autonomous; it owes almost everything of consequence to its roots in the religious history of Latin Christianity and its conflicts with various state formations. At the point I left off my discussion of the history of the late Roman Empire in the previous chapter, I noted that the religious and the political had merged into a single *respublica Christiania,* dominated by ecclesiastical institutions, such as the papacy. Papal power was "akin to that wielded today by what we call the state." (Oakley 2003, 6) The State of the Middle Ages was, in effect, a "transformed Church." This means that, in addition to *auctoritas,* the Church wielded *potestas* in a way it had not in the early centuries of the common era. Recall the collapse of the formula worked out by Pope Gelasius I. Thus, at least since the foundation of the Holy Roman Empire and the recognition of the Carolingian line by the popes, the Church too ruled in the world as a worldly power – armed with *potestas* like every other 'prince of this world.'

From as early as the fifth century, Francis Oakley claims that the "Church ceased to be a voluntary, private organization comparable to other social organizations and became instead a compulsory, all-inclusive, and coercive society comparable to what we call the state and, in its totality, well-nigh indistinguishable from it." (Oakley 2006, 94)

The situation in the Frankish-Latin Western Empire, then, contrasted with that prevailing in the Byzantine empire of the East. It is true that the Western emperors like Constantine, and Frankish Holy Roman Emperors too, ruled according to principles of a qualified limited sacral kingship, like their corresponding monarchs in the East. But, however divinely appointed and guided the Western emperors were believed to be, they did not administer sacraments. How different, then, the presumptions of the Eastern emperor, Leo III, who reminded the pope that "he himself though emperor, was still a priest." (Oakley 2006, 79) In the West, it is "the "kingly priesthood" of the Roman Church that became salient. The Church thus became the basis of "a monarchy of unprecedented type, a spiritual monarchy." (Dumont 1986a, 23–59, 50) Figgis even went so far as to claim that the divine right of kings was, in this way, first claimed by the pope. (Figgis 1998, 29)

But, despite the fact that in the Middle Ages the pope's combined *auctoritas* and *potestas* exceeded that of the emperor, the actual *practice* of obedience and submission suggested deeper disquiets. Therefore, although the pope held "supremacy over all kings and princes," this condition was always subject to uneasy contestation – mostly in practice, if not in terms of new doctrine. (Figgis 1998, 37) One example tells us a great deal about this uneasy arrangement. Henry III, Holy Roman Emperor (1039–56), dismissed three "rival claimants" to the papacy, and then appointed three others, the last being his own cousin! (Oakley 2006, 111) But, in a spectacular display of papal authority over the Holy Roman Emperors, his son, Henry IV (1056–1106), was excommunicated in a dispute with Gregory VII over the right to "invest" bishops. Henry repented his opposition, and petitioned the pope to relieve his excommunication by standing in the snow for three days outside the gates of the castle of Canossa in January of 1077. Henry was eventually reinstated by the pope, but as soon as he was, he resumed his violations! So, while we can see that the popes ruled, they also did so somewhat uneasily. This reflected the original ambivalent structural arrangements made between the pope and Charlemagne. In receiving his title as emperor from the pope, Charlemagne also asserted his "paramountcy" as well as his "duty not only to protect but to direct the Church." (Dumont 1986a, 23–59, 49)

The experience of the worldly rule of the popes in the Middle Ages was to mark all our thinking about power and politics thereafter. At its most extreme, this gives rise to right-wing German political philosopher Carl Schmitt's view that religion essentially determined our politics:

> All significant concepts of the theory of the state are secularized theological concepts not only because of their historical development – in which they were transferred from theology to the theory of the state, whereby, for example, the omnipotent God became the omnipotent lawgiver – but also because of their systematic structure, the recognition of which is necessary for a sociological consideration of these concepts. (Schmitt 2005b, 36)

But, while there is no need to go as far as Schmitt, one can learn from Figgis, in particular, that much of our politics is rooted in religion. Thus, the "sonorous phrases of the Declaration of Independence or the Rights of Man are … not an original discovery, they are the heirs of all the ages, the depository of the emotions and the thoughts of seventy generations of culture." (Figgis 1998, 30) The rules, so to speak, for wielding *potestas* were written by the popes as much as they were the result of imperial deeds. The actual fact of the worldly rule by a theoretically other-worldly institution, such as the Church, left its mark on Western traditions of practical sovereignty and political thought. (Oakley 1996, 60–110, 93)

8. What Constitutionalism Owes the Council of Constance

One stunning example of this ecclesiastical influence upon our fundamental secular institutions may be found in the institution of constitutionalism. Prominent among other evidence for such a legacy of intimacy between Church and State is the frequently celebrated influence of the Council of Constance (1414–18) – what historian Francis Oakley called the "most memorable general council held by the Latin Church." (Oakley 2003, 21) Called originally to end the embarrassment of Christendom having three simultaneously contending popes, and thus to resolve the Great Western Schism, the Council of Constance was occupied with weighty decisions. Finally, resolving the dispute among the contending popes in favor of one, the Council issued its summary document, the *Sacrosancta*. Significant for us is that modern historians have seen this ecclesiastical document as enunciating a principle that would give priority to both ecclesiological *and* secular constitutionalism. (Skinner 1978, 123) The Council's final statement asserted the rights of the council over against the papacy, and in effect, challenged any incipient absolutist notions of governance both in the Church and, by example, in the secular sphere as well. (Figgis 1998, 36) "In the religious sphere," the *Sacrosancta* "became a classic defense of the rights of the ... many against the claims of the one." (Ozment 1980, 157)

> This holy Council of Constance ... declares, first, that it is lawfully assembled in the Holy Spirit, that it constitutes a General Council, representing the Catholic Church, and that therefore it has its authority immediately from Christ; and that all men, of every rank and condition, including the pope himself, are bound to obey it ... (Bettenson 1970, 192–3, cited in Ozment 1980, 156)

Constance, and other examples of what is called 'conciliar' thought of the fifteenth century, lived on, despite setbacks and revivals of

119

papal authoritarianism into modern times – even to the extent that they also "exerted demonstrable influence upon the constitutional and resistance theorists of the sixteenth and seventeenth centuries." (Oakley 1996, 60–110, 93)

For enthusiasts of Constance, the council's decree determined the pope to be "in some sense a constitutional ruler," (Oakley 2003, 72) and in doing so, produced nothing short, says one prominent historian of the period, of "the most revolutionary official document in the history of the world." (Figgis 1998, 34) This document issuing from the Council of Constance, the *Sacrosancta,* was the first official statement of the "rights of the people" or "popular sovereignty" in the history of the West. The *Sacrosancta* of the early fifteenth century was, of course, 'populist' and 'democratic' in the way Magna Carta was "in the political sphere." In the long run, conciliarism set out the principle that "divine right" also resided in the people – that it was "inherent in the spiritual kingdom of the faithful." (Oakley 1962, 1–31, 31) That is also to say that while the *Sacrosancta* may not have been a full declaration of our modern notions of democracy and individual rights as found in the Declaration of Independence or the Rights of Man, the *Sacrosancta* moved things along in that direction.

There is every reason to think, therefore, that the lessons of Constance passed to the founders of the American and French republics by way of resistance theorists and constitutionalists of the seventeenth century. That "robust parliamentarian," Puritan William Prynne (1600–69), repeatedly cited the precedent of the Council of Constance in his efforts to assert the primacy of parliament over the absolutist pretensions of the English king. (Oakley 2003, 230) Contemporary historians, from Dale van Kley on the French Jansenists to Quentin Skinner on Calvinist resistance and revolution thinkers, have argued that Constance indirectly, but nonetheless indeed, gave birth to our own modern notion of "constitutionalism." (Skinner 1978, 123)

That, at least, constitutional scholars recognize the revolutionary nature of constitutional principles only affirms these historical judgments about the importance of the Council of Constance. Commenting on the *practicality* of American constitutionalism, a prominent American student of constitutional law recently remarked:

> The rejection of absolutism implicit in our constitutional structure may sometimes make our policies seem unprincipled. But, for the most of our history, it has encouraged the very process of information gathering, analysis, and argument that allows us to make better, if not perfect, choices, not only about the means to our ends but also about the ends themselves. (Obama 2006, 94)

Constitutionalism, on his view, then holds the place of an absolute, dare I say, 'religious' value, since it embodies the very "ends" of life itself. The absolute and unquestionable nature of our nation's commitment to constitutionalism has prompted that same man who would become the 44th president of the United States, Barack Obama, to declare: "Sometimes I imagined my work to be not so different from the work of the theology professors who taught across campus." (Obama 2006, 85)

I shall only note in passing here that, as one might expect, anthropologist Talal Asad refuses to attribute to religion, in this case, Christianity, any agency in constituting our present political ideas and institutions. Directing his jibes at an admittedly extreme proponent of this view, Carl Schmitt, Asad says: "One of the things in Carl Schmitt's political theology that I find myself dissatisfied with is his attempt to show that many secular political ideas are essentially Christian." (Scott 2006, 243–303, 285) May I say, however, that it is Asad who might perhaps pay more attention to the religious foundations of our modern American political institutions. Is it plausible that even after achieving their "Great Separation" from one another – after the modern severance of religious and political "arms" from one another – these two "arms," once joined so closely for long, should be utter strangers to one another? (Lilla 2008) It should be obvious that since our country grew out of historical processes characteristic of Western civilization, and that since

Western civilization was formed in critical ways by Christianity, the foundation of our country can hardly escape its own – at least Latin or Western – Christian history.

But here precisely is the rub, and where some of the nastier battles of current US 'culture wars' are joined. *In what sense* can, say, the United States be said substantially to be indebted to Christianity, such that our citizenship places us under obligations that can be said to be rooted in the history of Christianity in the West, and identified as such? If we are to believe the Christian Right, nothing short of a *belief* in God is required of all Americans in order to remain faithful to the American founding. As the Christian Right argues, do not the monotheistic beliefs of the founders, as formally codified in the Declaration of Independence's reference to "Nature's God" and the "Creator," settle the matter? One implication of my argument today is that the debate about the relation of our politics and religion in the United States is set on the wrong course. The Christian Right has simply been looking in the wrong places for evidence of the importance of religion in the American founding. It is not to core Christian beliefs that we should look to understand the transcendent values founding our nation. It is to *historically accidental* facts about Latin Christianity, such as conciliarism, that we should look in the search for the sources of our dedication to republican constitutionalism. Christianity could well have been quite otherwise than an institution based on representative and conciliar principles. While Christianity is inconceivable without Jesus, monotheism, and a number of other beliefs, one can well conceive of Christianity in which councils of the Church were never convened, and in which decisions were never made by councils, roughly representing the membership of the Church as a collective body. Indeed, "high Papalism" has done all in its power to erase the conciliarism that dominated the first thousand years of Christian history from the collective memory of Christianity. That "high Papalism" has not succeeded in this erasure, and that conciliarism represents both the bulk of the Reformation tradition as well as the leading edge of progressive Roman Catholicism, in the figure of such resisters as Swiss theologian Hans Küng, speak eloquently to the political nature of this ongoing struggle to define the nature of sovereignty in the Church. (Küng 2007)

Thus, to say, as I have, that our politics shows the mark of the past because our commitment to republican constitutionalism derives from Christian conciliarism is not to oblige anyone to commitment to any essential Christian belief. It is, instead, to recognize the concrete institutional historical processes that have given us our constitutional and representative politics. Autocrats of all ages have eagerly seized upon the paradigmatic and legitimating model of papal absolutism to support their own absolutisms. Given what I have argued, those committed to constitutional and republican forms of government can then feel confident that having recourse to the history of Latin Christianity can likewise support democratic political institutions. Far from making Christians of all of us, it should make historians – and historians of *religion,* I might add – of all of us. In that sense, grasping how and why aspects of our politics are not separable from religion demands no religious commitment, only a belief in the reality of historical processes and institutions. Affirming modern innovations does not require denying ancient foundations. And that is one reason why our politics cannot be said to be autonomous, freed – in our case – from religion.

9. The Emergence of the Political …
from the Religious

But this account leaves us naturally to wonder how the political separated itself off from the theological. If the Middle Ages were characterized by an *interpenetration* or *confusion* of worldly and other-worldy, of Empire and Church, of kingly and priestly *auctoritas* and *potestas,* how did the two sorts of institutions disengage from each other in the way we now take to be *natural* and *normal?* What had to transpire for those who felt that an institution like the Church should be pushed aside to make way for civil institutions autonomous of it? What events and conditions, then, gave rise to the idea that there was such an autonomous realm as politics – a realm that monopolized *potestas,* the use of force, and so on? How did "politics" and "the political" emerge? What made the distinctive thought of a Machiavelli, Luther, Hobbes, or Rousseau possible, as it were? What made their relegation of religion, as we have seen earlier in our "interrogation of 'religion'," variously to the domain of the 'private', individual, or internal possible? What, correspondingly, made their assumption and assertion of the political, understood as enthroning power as *potestas* and the conflict model as the highest form of social and public life, follow necessarily from the grounds of their thought? How, therefore, did the ideal of an autonomous politics, presumed and empowered by their thinking, emerge?

This will also be to ask the more paradoxical question of how the "religion of the State" emerged from and replaced the religion of the Church. How, despite the deliberate attempts by many of the political thinkers of the age to purge religion from the public realm, did it *unintentionally* return under the name of 'politics'? How, despite their attempts to isolate religion to the internal, private domain of the individual conscience and thus to identify the public domain with politics, did they only succeed, perhaps against their own wishes, in sanctifying politics? How, despite their attempts to eliminate the sacred from public life, did they *unknowingly* only succeed in transferring the "halo of sanctity" to the "temporal sovereign" from the ecclesiastical? (Figgis 1998, 72) How did civil power come to have many of the salient features of ecclesiastical institutions, like the Church, despite the best efforts of many to prevent this from happening? How did the State come to feel it 'natural' to make "paramount claims of an organized society upon the allegiance of its members"? (Figgis 1998, 96) How did the State become worthy of "sacrifice," and in many senses, come to be regarded as superior to religion, even though it simply assumed the role religion had once had? Why is its authority – *auctoritas* – over life and death virtually unquestioned, as much as any *ex cathedra* pronouncement

124

from the Vatican? Why, for example, does an otherwise worldly institution, such as the State, assume a religious character by becoming the focus of absolute obedience? Why does the nation-state as well arrogate unto itself the monopoly of the use of *potestas* – force and violence? How, therefore, did the absolute inviolability of the unity of religion yield to the assumption of the unity of the State, of the sacred nature of its boundaries and territorial integrity, of the absolute taboo against a 'state within a state,' and so on?

10. Machiavelli and Luther: Critical Contributions to the Autonomy of Politics

Answers to this long list of questions are to be found, in part, in an equally long series of lessons drawn from the suppression of the values asserted at the Council of Constance (1414–18). It is well beyond the scope of this book to detail the entire story of this transformation of Western society. Aquinas, Calvin, Ockham, Locke, Grotius, Pufendorf, the Jesuits, and others play important roles in this story. It would demand another book itself to do justice to all of them. Instead, I choose to mark some significant moments in the story. And, while it greatly oversimplifies matters to make so much of reactions to failure of the Council of Constance, there is enough truth in this claim to identify some of the impelling factors behind the emergence of the political. Let me mark some major mileposts along the way to the assumption of the autonomy of politics by referring to them briefly with some 'thumbnail' sketches of major thinkers who figured in this shift of consciousness in the West. Here, I single out Machiavelli and Luther as having made signal contributions both to the idea of the autonomy of politics and, paradoxically as well, to its concomitant sacrality.

First, then, to Machiavelli. According to the standard narrative, Machiavelli is posed as an evil genius acting out of motives drawn from thin air. We now know much better than this, thanks to a host of scholars. (Berlin 1979, 25–79) Some of these argue that Machiavelli may have drawn his models of absolutism for *The Prince* from preexisting absolutisms. Is it unrealistic to think that Machiavelli may have been inspired by the absolutist Church itself? Machiavelli may have thought that a "new absolutism" was appropriate because in the crushing of the constitutionalism of Constance, the Church, among other institutions of Machiavelli's acquaintance, had shown very well what absolutism at work looked like. (Dumont 1986b, 60–103, 71) But, whatever the original source of Machiavelli's ideas, *The Prince* boldly reasoned that an autonomous political sphere was independent of the religious or moral one. It was only by ruling according to the supreme principle of 'reasons of state' that a ruler could hope to preserve his realm. Attempting to govern the state by the Christian ethics appropriate to the individual would only bring ruin to the realm. In our own time, these sentiments will strike a familiar tone. Along with the concept of 'reasons of state,' of course, comes the notion of 'state' as itself something separate and distinctive in its existence. Quentin Skinner argues that in Machiavelli we begin to see such an emergence of 'state' – significantly from the idea of the 'state' as the condition of *status* of the body of the prince. In this conception of 'state,' Machiavelli articulates the notion of the emergence of politics in a "recognizably modern sense." (Skinner 1978, 354) But, citing Skinner, Tim Fitzgerald points out that it is really to the French humanist Jean Bodin that we should look for an articulation of a "conceptualization of the State as a locus of power which can be institutionalized in a variety of ways, and which remains distinct from and superior to both its citizens and their magistrates." (Skinner 1978, 356)

Witness, for instance, how the political philosopher and doyen of "political realism," Hans Morgenthau, gives voice to a purely Machiavellian point of view regarding the possible role of Christian ethics in modern politics:

The moral problem of politics is posed by the inescapable discrepancy between the commands of Christian teaching, of Christian ethics, and the requirements of political success. It is impossible, if I may put it in somewhat extreme and striking terms, to be a success-ful politician and a good Christian. (Morgenthau 1962, 97–110, 102)

Thus, political decisions should be made on political grounds alone, not religious ones. Coercive force then knows no limits other than those of countervailing force, or some shrewd calculation of advantage in limiting the use of *potestas*. Politics was thus autonomous of morality or religion, and was governed by its own rules – the rules governing the advantageous play of manipulation, coercive force, and cunning – the rule of domination as a value.

Thomas Hobbes, in this sense, can be seen as putting his own twist on much of what Machiavelli stands for, especially his obsession with the political. For Hobbes, we are, rather, social beings only at the "political level." And we are made into such social beings by the coercive power of the "transcendent Ruler." Indeed, the Ruler insures that the social is thus "restricted to the political" for Hobbes. (Dumont 1986b, 60–103, 84–5) The overall effect of this ascendancy of politics over any other domain of life, including religion, is to promote politics to the place religion once occupied in society as a whole. *'Potestas,'* coercive force, becomes the supreme value, and is embodied as the essence of the State, since the State alone monopolizes coercive force. (Celtel 2005, 109) Again, Morgenthau, in effect, brings another historical thinker, such as Hobbes, up to date in articulating his influential "realist" theory of politics:

I would … maintain that it is particularly difficult to be a Christian in politics, because the aim of man in politics is to dominate another man, to use a man as an instrument, as a means to his ends; and this is a direct denial of Judaeo-Christian ethics. The political act is in a specific, particularly acute sense incompatible with Christian ethics, in a sense in which the non-political act is free. (Morgenthau 1962, 97–110, 111)

So much for anyone foolish enough to believe that Christian loving-kindness could be a value in governance.

127

Next, to Luther. Given that the union of papal and imperial dominion had been responsible for silencing the conciliar spirit of the Council of Constance, reaction to it could have broad consequences. Chief among them was the way Martin Luther bought the freedom of the political at the price of suppressing the ecclesiastical. The reaction against the medieval notion of the Church as supreme corresponded to Luther's counter-assertion of the State as autonomous of papal power – and in time, of *any* power. The political was autonomous because the prince was free of the *potestas* and *auctoritas* of the Church. (Figgis 1998, 67) Luther effectively, thereby, destroyed the principle of the "two swords" by which the Empire and Church both wielded *potestas* according to the medieval formula. Instead, Luther sought to install a "godly prince," who alone would wield the power of coercive force by right. (Figgis 1998, 65)

While Luther was freeing the prince from papal domination, he was also raising up the prince and the State to levels heretofore reserved only for the pope and the Church – to the level of divine right and absolutism. Concurring in this judgment, Quentin Skinner says that "there is no doubt that the main influence of Lutheran political theory in early modern Europe lay in the direction of encouraging and legitimating the emergence of unified and absolutist monarchies." (Skinner 1978) In this sense, the doctrine of the divine right of kings inherent in Luther's thought amounted to an assertion of absolute lay supremacy over the ecclesiastical. It claimed that the authority of the prince came directly from God and, therefore, that "political society" had an "inherent right" to exist as such. There can be little more emphatic assertions of the autonomy (as well as supremacy) of the political than we meet with Luther. Figgis concludes by claiming that Luther's legacy for politics is not only in terms of principles, but also in terms of the ultimate superiority of a particular form of social organization – the State or political society – "the unity and universality and essential rightness of the sovereign territorial State, and the denial of every extra-territorial or independent communal form of life."

(Figgis 1998, 70) The prince now wields the "civil sword," and he and the State are free from – *autonomous of* – every other human institution. They answer only directly to God. (Figgis 1998, 63)

But, if the State now dominates public space, we might now recall what we noted earlier happens to religion. Luther's answer is simple and compelling in terms of the logic he has worked out. Religion departs the 'public square' and becomes a matter of the private personal conscience and confined to the Church. It is something performed either within the confines of one's own soul or together in intimate privacy of church fellowship, but restricted to Sundays. We get nothing less than the "naked public square" made notable by the criticism of it issuing from convert *from* Lutheranism Father Richard John Neuhaus! (Neuhaus 1984) The counterpart to Luther's making the State "visible," so to speak, is that religion thus becomes 'invisible,' in the sense that religion becomes largely internal – a matter of the private conscience – without rights to a voice in the 'public square,' or it becomes 'separate' from the state and power. (Figgis 1998, 68) Religion, in the form of a social body, vacates the political realm of the 'public square,' and leaves the prince in charge over religion. "All coercive authority was vested in the prince by Divine Right; that the power of the State was absolutely vested in him; that no other separate organization could exist except by his fiat, or by his delegation … No real social unities are to exist apart from the State." (Figgis 1998, 69)

In respect to Luther's privatization and individualization of religion and deification of the State, we can see Rousseau as carrying the effort a step further. Although Rousseau does advance the idea of a "civil religion," and thus seems to place religion into a rightful place in the 'public square,' the source of this religion is not the transcendent God of theistic religion, but a kind of expression of the General Will, the voice of the "People." By nature, people, then, may be individuals, and not social beings. But once a social contract is 'signed' as it were, the "General Will" embodied therein creates a totality out of a potentially unruly mass of human wills. That totality, known as the "People," alone is sovereign. And politics is its voice in the world. Since there can be no higher authority than the General Will, it attains a level of transcendence similar to the Ruler in Hobbes' vision of the properly ordered social whole. In both cases, as with both Machiavelli and Luther, politics emerges as autonomous and supreme.

11. Foucault's Fault II: 'Everything Is Political'

I have just been arguing that an interrogation of 'politics' in the West reveals that what we take to be the political has been shaped — indeed defined — by a very special sort of history. This makes it hard, if not impossible, to go along with the likes of Hans Morgenthau, who asserts the autonomy of politics, not only in the face of all other social activities and standards, but also over against historical differences. On the contrary, I have been arguing that we need to historicize such a putatively autonomous 'politics.' The political has been an emergent category in the West. In the future, it might well lose its emergent autonomy, in the sense of being thought more appropriately subordinated to, or compromised by, other domains of human behavior, such as religion or economics. What are clerisies or theocracies but such schemes in which strictly political considerations are hemmed in and/or informed by religion, such as in the Islamic Republic of Iran? A chief complaint of the left has been that such a compromise has already been made. To them, in liberal societies, market freedom has been paid with the coin of political control. The market may be autonomous but politics has lost its autonomy. I do not deny, however, that the political does retain some distinctiveness, even as it overlaps with other parts of the human world. It thus makes sense, for example, to speak of *both* political and religious *auctoritas* or authority, since they are proper to both the domains of politics and religion. But that autonomy of the political remains a contingent matter of our history.

While there is commonsense consensus that the political necessarily involves affairs of state, others have argued that this is perhaps too *narrow* a designation. What if we were to revisit one of Morgenthau's "six points," and embrace something of the spirit of his view that "politics, like society in general, is governed by objective laws that have their roots in *human nature* …" and, further that "human nature, in which the laws of politics have their roots, *has not changed* …"? (My emphases; Morgenthau 1965, 4) If we were to do this, then we would generalize politics across the whole range of human actions, and have little interest in, say, things like the unique emergence of the nation-state, the transformation of the Church into the State, the relegation of the religious to the private sphere while the State dominates the public realm, and so on.

From a negative point of view, this, in effect, is where the thinking of Michel Foucault leads. The "fruitfulness of focusing on the State," Foucault believes, "has been exhausted."(Foucault 1977b, 183–93, 188) Speaking more positively, Foucault might say that he seeks to redefine and enrich what we should mean by 'the political.' Thus, he says that "one impoverishes the question of power if one poses it solely in terms of legislation and constitution, in terms solely of the state, and the state apparatus." (Foucault 1977a, 146–65, 158) Instead of concerns about the religious origins of the State, such as I explored, Foucault would prefer to see politics as involving "a more complicated, dense and pervasive a set of laws." (Foucault 1977a, 146–65, 158) Foucault seeks to map just such a "set of relations of force in a society." And, from this broad vantage point, he defines "politics" as a "strategy for co-ordinating and directing these relations." As such,

> Every relation of force implies at each moment a relation of power … and every power relation makes a reference, as its effect, but also as its condition of possibility, to a political field of which it forms a part. To say that 'everything is political' is to affirm this ubiquity of relations of force and their immanence in a political field … (Foucault 1977b, 183–93, 189)

Ironically, however, Foucault's rendering of everything as political only makes his conception of politics all the more fierce and aggravated. For him, politics is not about states and bodies politic, but about the "micro-fascisms of everyday life." And, in its reduced scale, Foucault's 'politics' does not, however, reduce the ferocity and bellicosity of the conflicts found there. For Foucault, then, power, politics, and war seem only different aspects of the same thing:

> None of the political struggles, the conflicts waged over power, with power, for power, the alterations in the relation of forces, the favouring of certain tendencies, the reinforcements, etc., that come about within this 'civil' peace – that none of these phenomena in a political system should be interpreted except as a continuation of war. (Foucault 1980, 90)

Such a point of view commits Foucault to the embrace of what he acknowledges is an "inversion of the Clausewitzian aphorism." While, for Clausewitz, "war is the pursuit of politics by other means," for Foucault, "politics is the pursuit of war by other means." (Foucault 1980, 90) For Foucault, therefore, the entire field of agency collapses into the political, and ultimately the warlike. "The role of political power … is perpetually to reinscribe this relation [war] through a form of unspoken warfare."(Foucault 1980, 90) Foucault thus sees the real meaning of "politics" as a "sanctioning and upholding of the disequilibrium of forces that was displayed in war …" (Foucault 1980, 90) Unlike the vagaries of meaning we saw as typical of 'religion' or 'power,' Foucault's idea of politics and power could not be more precise.

Foucault's visions of power and politics as the property of "innumerable points" and extensive "networks" of force have their value. He makes us take note of the subtle kinds of conflict that can afflict life in the world, often at very intimate range, such as in sex. But shifting attention away from the State has its drawbacks. For critics like Michael Walzer, Foucault's aversion of his gaze from the State to the level of the "micro-fascism of everyday life" ignores the fact that the "political regime, the sovereign state" in which we live, in many ways, sets the conditions for everyday life. Walzer and I (I might add) seek to bring out how the nation serves as an ultimate context for meaning and belonging for individuals, how the State plays a role in informing what our most intimate relations can be. As Walzer puts it:

> For it is the state that establishes the general framework within which all other disciplinary institutions operate. It is the state that holds open or shuts down the possibility of local resistance. The agents of every disciplinary institution strive, of course, to extend their reach and augment their discretionary power. Ultimately, it is only state power that can stop them. Every act of local resistance is an appeal for political or legal intervention from the centre. (Walzer 1986, 51–68, 66)

It should be obvious from my treatment of the Empire and Church relations and my reckoning with the emergence of politics that I take Walzer's side in this difference of priority. We cannot understand, for example, something as critical in today's world as the idea of the secular – of how religion gets relegated to the private realm and dismissed from the secular domain of the 'public square' – unless we approach politics at the level of the State. To take the matter right into Foucault's 'court,' we cannot understand such intimately experienced aspects of life such as the public/private distinction itself, unless we grasp how our history has made it so. That, at the very least, is why we need to go well past thinking that 'everything is political' to understanding the political itself.

12. The Hidden Fascism of Thinking that Everything Is Political

Another reason we should resist thinking that everything is politics, and worse yet a politics that is basically war, is because thinking so fails fully to appreciate the risks involved. We would like to imagine that this kind of sentiment can be kept under control for the 'good' progressive purposes we favor. We would like to think that exposing the pervasiveness of politics in the sense of the micro-fascism of everyday life will aid and abet liberationist goals. In many, many cases it will. But, it is worth reminding ourselves that the critique of liberalism that is so much a part of current liberationist thought, for instance, by Talal Asad and Michel Foucault, may not so easily be contained. Indeed, it was at the heart of Nazism, to mention only one totalitarian system thus constructed. Here, the words of famous German right-wing legal philosopher Carl Schmitt should be given heed. Schmitt provocatively notes that "One seldom finds a clear definition of the political." (Schmitt 2005a, 20) Yet, any hesitation behind this statement would not be long-lived. Schmitt not only embraces politics wholeheartedly, but he also takes to heart a model of politics as warfare. *'Potestas'* stands as his paramount value. "The specific political distinction to which political actions and motives can be reduced is that between friend and enemy," says Schmitt. (Schmitt 2005a, 26) Celebrating the idea of politics as a kind of blood sport, Schmitt vents his contempt for liberalism – as his active connections with National Socialism in the 1930s would suggest he would. Thus, Schmitt pours out his contempt for so-called 'bourgeois politics,' the politics of parliamentary compromises and negotiation. Politics simply cannot be domesticated in this way, because it is about taking sides. For Schmitt, politics is about the "possibility of dying for what was the determining quality of being human." (Strong 2007, ix–xxi, xvi) A strong sense of 'we' is required for a healthy politics, so that the friend/enemy opposition may be sharpened to the hilt. Further, expanding on the conflict model so essential to his concept of politics, Schmitt declares that "to the enemy concept belongs the ever-present possibility of combat." (Schmitt 2005a, 32) Chillingly, Schmitt adds: "A world in which the possibility of war is utterly eliminated, a completely pacified globe would be a world without the distinction of friend and enemy and hence a world without politics." (Schmitt 2005a, 35) Schmitt wants no part of a world devoid of politics; he actively approves of one in which everything is political.

13. Public and Private: No Absolute Line of Demarcation

However creative and illuminating Foucault's expansion of the reference of 'politics' has been, I believe it has tilted too much to a harsh conflict model of human life, and in the process has potentially sidestepped important lines of inquiry. There is life after Foucault, and living it largely depends on interrogating those terms that Foucault does not – 'power' and 'politics.' Thus, while the ease and prevalence of our talking in this unexamined way *with* terms like 'power' or 'politics' has created open space for all sorts of liberationist work, we pay a price for its conceptual openness. When, as I have argued in the previous chapter, the term 'power' embraces everything from simple 'agency,' at the more colorless end of the spectrum, to 'domination,' at the darker end, can we really be talking about the same thing? Similarly, when we have a politics about virtually *everything* under the sun, are we, similarly, thinking any more clearly, or indeed less dangerously, as my reference to Carl Schmitt suggests? When the entire social domain is reduced to the political, leaving out, just to mention one, the domain of civil society, we are in the grip of a kind of hegemonic imperialism over our thinking.

What ultimately follows for the prospects and character of human life if we hold to the oft-heard declaration that 'the personal is political'? While what counts as 'public' and 'private' will vary in different circumstances, what happens if we abolish the distinction in the way the slogan, 'the personal is the political,' demands of us? What would happen to the way we might want to live if certain domains considered 'private' were made 'public' by being made political? In years past, and still indeed in various places, wife-beating or certain forms of corporal punishment of one's own children were deemed exclusively 'private' domestic matters outside the scope of governmental regulation. By contrast, it is commonplace today that a majority or near-majority of our fellow citizens believe that many behaviors historically once considered suitable for public – political – regulation, such as same sex relations and religion, now are widely regarded as belonging to the personal or 'private' domain. This classification as 'private' accomplishes many things – chief among them perhaps is to make them exempt from regulation by political forces. What goes on sexually in the bedroom between consenting adults, or what goes on religiously among consenting church members – for the most part, at least – is free of public, that is, political regulation. A good part of the 'abortion debate' seems to be about drawing acceptable *boundaries* between public and private. Where does the private domain of the pregnant woman begin and end and the public interests of the State end and begin, respectively? In this, the privacy of domains of adult sex and religion are like ads promoting Las Vegas holidays there – 'holidays' from any sort of public or political regulation – which boldly announce: "what goes on here, stays here." While we may differ among ourselves ideologically as to which acts belong to the category of the personal and private over against the public and political, we would, it seems, be in accord that the distinction should remain. By excluding some acts from politics as 'personal,' we agree, despite ideological differences, that it is a good thing to secure a degree of freedom for the things we prefer to do – despite how we may disagree in other respects. (Minogue 1995, 5) Thus, at the very least, the determination to see politics in everything, such as in asserting that 'the personal is political,' exposes attitudes that bear watching. Ironically, these are the attitudes of Foucault's 'Panopticon' and its constant surveillance of human behavior. They are inconsistent with our desire to maintain a freedom of thought and action that people of different opposing ideological stripes likewise seek to varying degrees.

14. Resisting the Panopticon

It is in this spirit of resistance to the all-seeing eye of the Panopticon that I write this chapter seeking to expose the constructed nature of 'politics.' Because seeing things as political is so much a part of our 'natural' way of seeing things in the West, it takes a special effort to step back and appreciate what we are. I have not written this chapter, however, to dismiss politics, or to imagine that it can be simply thought away – but only to see it for what and where in human life it is, or should be. In this sense, I have stood as well, although critically, with those thinkers who stress the existence of politics in a variety of atypical domains of human life. (Strenski 1987; Strenski 1993a, 180–201; Strenski 1993b, 166–79; Strenski 1998a, 116–26; Strenski 1998b, 345–68) While trying to resist an overly politicized view of human affairs, I thus stand with those who oppose anyone who thinks that politics can everywhere be ignored. Thus, politics is *some*where in human life, but that does not mean it is, or should be, *every*where there in equal measure.

Perhaps it may be easier to grasp my discomfort with the pervasiveness of politics by appealing to the same way our lives have been commodified – in the way that economic values pervade the way we look at life, especially in places that we imagine they do not belong, such as our social relations. Perhaps nothing is so disconcerting or disenchanting about personal relationships as the discovery that the relationship was based only upon a calculation of material advantage to one's partner. How often are potential partners selected for their prospects as successful money earners? My nephews and nieces in the 'dating world' tell me that it is routine that some men will only get interested in a particular woman if they know she is well established in a career that fetches a handsome income, or from a moneyed family, or unlikely to drain their own economic resources. Likewise, other men friends in that world tell similar tales of how feminine interest is piqued by the same factors. All of a sudden, my financially successful, but squat and prematurely balding male friends find swarms of available women round them, while their classically attractive male mates, pulling modest assistant professor's salaries, are baffled at the spectacle! It is not only power, but also money, that is notoriously the most powerful aphrodisiac!

137

In a way, nothing is new here. People have always 'used' people. But what is depressing about this state of affairs to many of us is that it seems to some to *typify* how human relations are now more generally conditioned. What depresses many is the sense of the normative character of making the calculation of economic gain the *basis* for entering into social relations. What makes such a world look bleak is that the market now seems to have shaped the most intimate shared values of our society. Again, it is not just the *individual* case of someone marrying for money and so on that undermines our optimism about the human prospect, but the indication that this behavior has a general and overarching application. Everybody, or nearly everybody, goes about entering into what should be intimate, life-long relationships based upon *economic calculations,* rather than on friendship, deep emotional attachments, mutual regard for character in the other, and so on.

Having said many skeptical things about the pretensions of politics, nothing I have said in this chapter should lead one to assume that I harbor a dismal view of politics. Politics in the nation-state is what it is. The point about becoming aware of our *belief* in the autonomy of politics is to raise our awareness to a level sufficient to see this is a *belief* – an assumption made within our culture, but perhaps, like Evans-Pritchard's Nuer, not in others. Indeed, in showing how indebted our politics is to religion in the West, I have tried to show how our belief in the autonomy of politics was bought along with that of religion. I do not then share the cynicism about politics so fashionable today. Such disparaging judgments as 'That's just politics!' trade on the presumed self-evidence that the term names something slimy and despicable. Similarly, in the letter section of a recent edition of the *Los Angeles Times,* a large, bold-type, headline to a missive trashing politics as essentially corrupt read tellingly, "Typical Politician." (Decker 2008, A15)

What I hope that I have shown in radically interrogating 'politics' is how bound up with religion it has been, and still is. Neither is necessarily good *nor* bad. They have been, and in some cases still are, vital combinations of *potestas* and *auctoritas,* unions of sheer coercive force and less tangible, but just as real, authority. Thus, it would be interesting to see if the same people who think that religion is necessarily good, likewise believe that politics is bad. Despite the intense engagement in politics by someone like the Reverend Pat Robertson, we find just such a person well in the grip of the double-sided cliché that religion is good, and politics bad – well, at least some religions. Thus, Robertson has argued that Islam is bad, precisely because it is a political movement. "We have to recognize that Islam is not a religion," said Robertson to the astonishment of anyone who knows the slightest things about religion. Instead, said he, "It is a worldwide political movement meant on domination of the world." (Robertson 2007)

This kind of thinking about politics, while not as extreme as Robertson's, can be found as well among many who consider themselves enlightened and worldly. They fall prey to Talal Asad's critique of the prevailing concept of religion among many scholars and writers, not to mention many common citizens. (Asad 1993) For them, 'real' Christianity, like 'real' Islam, is 'interior.' They are things of morality or the 'heart' – something that can be discerned in a person by testing the quality of their intentions or beliefs. If we know that a person's 'heart' is good, we can know that the whole person and their behavior are fundamentally good as well, even if they stray from the ideal. The assumption of such opposition rests on some religious convictions particular to religious beliefs that grew out of the history of religion in the West that remains today much taken for granted and very widespread, especially in the United States. Although this trend of religious thinking is perhaps most conspicuously seen in the Wesleyan tradition, its roots in what scholars have called the "religion of the heart," or the religion of sincerity and enthusiasm, run deep into the groundwork of Western modernity. (Knox 1950)

15. Afterword: The Autonomy of 'Politics' and the Nation-State

In our own time, we do need to grasp the fact that the historical processes that produced the political as an autonomous realm culminate in the nation-state. The 'State' as "transformed Church" is our very own ideal of the nation or nation-state. As a result, nation-states will reek of religion. Whatever else they may be, nations are, like religions, meaning-making entities of grand and transcendent sorts, creating an aura of sacredness about all their central doings. Despite globalization running apace for many years, the nation remains the principal supra-individual entity in whom individuals find a meaning greater than themselves. Thus far at least, for all the efforts of universal cosmopolitan 'humanity' to rally people to common human causes, it has yet to outdo the nation (or religion, proper) in calling forth the loyalty of people and in getting them to lay down their lives for it. The nation is thus regarded as worthy of the ultimate gift of the individuality of its citizens – a giving up of one's life in civic 'sacrifices' such as war. Benedict Anderson has argued that the readiness of individuals to kill others and to sacrifice themselves can only be understood in terms of the religious nature of fellowship achieved by the nation-state – that place where religion and nation are not usefully distinguishable. (Anderson 1991) People do not sacrifice themselves for "administrative units," such as the EU, but lately for nations – whether actual or imagined – like Bosnia, Serbia, Ireland, Israel, and Palestine, or, I would add, potentially for religions like Islam or Christianity. In some cases, the nation-state and religion compete for highest loyalty. In some cases, the competition favors the nation over religion – because, as we know, it simply assumed the role religion had once had. Its authority – *auctoritas* – over life and death is virtually unquestioned, as much as the *magisterium* of the Vatican is for observant Catholics. The State likewise monopolizes the use of *potestas,* coercive force, violence, and such, and thus can enforce absolute obedience as popes of the Middle Ages could with their own armies. Its unity as a State is deemed sacred; its boundaries and territorial integrity are sacrosanct, the transgression of which constitutes a universally recognized *casus belli,* and so on. The State's flags, monuments, anthems, and such partake of the same transcendent religious glow of the nation as sacred being. The reason that nationalism is so saturated in religious meaning is that "administrative units" do not create meaning while, in a sense, religions and nations do nothing but create meaning – however gruesome it may be.

Let me then conclude this book by just such an example of an anguishing and gruesome quest for meaning and nationhood – the case of the pursuit of Palestinian nationhood by the so-called suicide bombers of the Muslim Middle East.

5

Testing Interrogations of 'Religion,' 'Power,' and 'Politics'
Human Bombers and the Authority of Sacrifice in the Middle East

21. *I hate your religious festivals; I cannot stand them!*
22. *When you bring me burnt offerings and grain offerings, I will not accept them: I will not accept the animals you have fattened to bring me as offerings.* (Amos, 5: 21–2)

And do not kill yourselves (nor kill one another). Surely, Allah is Most Merciful to you. (Qur'an: Surah 4:29)

Let those fight in the way of Allah who sell the life of this world for the other. Whoso fighteth in the way of Allah, be he slain or be he victorious, on him We shall bestow a vast reward. (Qur'an: Surah 4:74)

1. Is 'Suicide' Bombing Religious?

After so relentless an interrogation of 'religion,' 'power,' and 'politics' in the previous chapters, readers will rightly want to see if I have actually done anything to enhance our understanding of the practical realities of religion, power, and politics. Put to the test, for example, can these revamped ways of *'seeing'* religion, power, and politics help make greater sense as we *'look'* on something as acutely vexing as 'suicide' bombings in the Middle East? Showing that it can will be the substance of this chapter. Indeed, this phenomenon spurred a larger strategic effort to inquire whether present-day Middle Eastern Muslim 'suicide' bombing, or 'human bombing,' does more than attempt to project *power,* and exert direct *'political'* force, but also reveals something that might be called a 'religious' dimension as well. In particular, I believe that what we have learned by interrogating critical terms such as 'religion,' 'power,' and 'politics' can help us think about and understand human bombing in the Middle East in a far richer way than had been possible before. To be sure, there may be other construals of religion, power, and politics that may differ from mine. Other interrogators may devise other questions for interrogation. They may also enrich our understanding of often refractory religio-political phenomena, like suicide bombers in the Middle East, in their own ways. So be it. But in this chapter I should like to present how my interrogation of basic categories like religion, power, and politics can enrich our understanding of this anguishing contemporary phenomenon that seems to be both a religious and political phenomenon at the same time.

Take 'religion' first. Just how could a religious dimension of human bombing be construed or defined? If 'religion' be involved here, how might we pick it out? Is human bombing in the Middle East 'religious' in any commonsense or everyday sense of the term? Yes, Islam is invoked in cases. But perhaps Pat Robertson was right that such an invocation of Islam really masks a deeper non-religious nature? Perhaps politicians or other unscrupulous persons are only *using* Islam for other than 'religious' reasons? Perhaps, therefore, Islam is just *used* as a 'tool' or handy label or excuse for something totally different than Islam the religion? To those who say, moreover, that human bombing in the Middle East is religious, do they also say it is necessarily good or bad? How does it, further, fit with the idea that religion is just about having certain beliefs, such as a belief in the existence of God, and God's transcendent dictates? How could the religion *in* human bombing, so to speak, be something essentially internal and private, when it is so obviously a public act? How could it also be 'religious,' given that it is also not something remote from public life and politics? As for the 'power' in human bombing, in what does it consist? Is 'power' a unified field of human agency here, or does the 'power' in human bombing consist in a complex of perhaps qualitatively different constituents? Is the 'power' of human bombers only, therefore, the 'power' of raw political power, coercive force, or *potestas?* Or do the facts require us to reexamine our prejudices and make room for 'power' in the sense of *auctoritas* – power as a kind of social – 'religious' – force? And, if we do so, can we see religion projecting 'power' in this sense – even in the political sphere? Finally, 'politics.' On the one side is an older, entrenched, and narrow way of thinking about 'politics' as proper to the State and its 'party politics'; on the other is the newly entrenched, and much broader, way of talking about 'politics,' associated with Michel Foucault, that ignores the State and sees 'politics' as a diffuse and pervasive quality of human life.

In the course of this book, I think I have developed another way of talking about 'power' and 'politics' that necessarily demands that we think about 'religion' along with them, but not subordinated to them. I have been trying to enable people to deepen their understandings of human life by seeing a 'religious' dimension in current (and past) events of politics and power. That has been part of the theoretical strategy I have been pursuing from the start. This chapter is then devoted to testing whether distinguishing a 'religious' feature in so-called suicide bombing in today's Middle East helps us achieve that broader understanding. Let me then start with the most obvious of all questions about suicide bombing: In what ways, if at all, does it make sense to call suicide bombing in the Middle East a *religious* phenomenon?

2. Making Too Much of Religion in 'Suicide' Bombing: 'Islamofascism'

Now, it requires no argument to persuade most people that the human bombings that we have recently witnessed in the Muslim Middle East have been *political* acts – projections of power as *potestas*.

And most people would think that it hardly needs to be proven that they contain a substantial *religious* element, as well, although those who think that religion is 'good' might balk. (Appleby 2002; Kelsay 2002) There is a kind of 'commonsense' that says that since Islam is a 'religion,' and most, if not all, human bombers have been Muslims, there is something peculiarly Islamic about human bombing in the Middle East. Moreover, the human bombers are widely believed to have been motivated or directed by Islamic beliefs or Quranic scriptural dictates to fight against oppression and for liberation of Muslim populations. Playing into this scenario, the fighters themselves make this abundantly clear in their publications, whether to the press or even in video form: that they fight both *for* Islam and *with* Islam. The human bombers imagine that they are recapitulating the sacred archetypes of their religious heroes, and so on, by imitating the examples set by their heroes, such as Hussein, Ali, the Prophet Muhammad, and others.

Maybe, within the context of their own Muslim traditions, the human bombers are like that? In their adherence to religious models, they might remind us of people who slap "WWJD" on the bumpers of their cars as only the latest in a long tradition of defining the Christian ideal as being "Christ-like." But, of course, this slogan begs the question of *which* Christ one has in mind. Jesus meek and mild, 'like a little child,' or the Jesus to come of the murderous Book of Revelation? It is no different for Muslims regarding their heroes. Thus, the human bombers might remind us of our own, more familiar, local American circumstances of radical protest against abortion clinics. The biblical injunction of the fifth commandment against killing informs the attempts by some 'Pro-Life' groups to save fetal lives by preventing the procedure, but too often, the same 'Pro-Life' groups see no contradiction in murdering the adult medical staff performing it. In an analogous way, the human bombers see themselves as asserting moral standards of dignity taught by a given religious tradition, even though their 'bombing' eventuates in the murder of innocents. In a far less extreme – not to mention non-violent – version, those following the biblical refrain, "let my people go!" not only announce a fight inspired *by* Christianity, but also one *for* a Christian vision of the just society. Little wonder, then, why trying to think about human bombing – short of moral denunciation or uncritical praise – causes such wrenching torment. My point is that whatever else may be true, most people see human bombing in the Middle East with Islam and religion written all over it.

Yet, in the West, we have probably made far too much (and, para-doxically, too little, as we will see) of the connection between human bombings and religion – and with Islam in particular. I am sure that readers will recognize the Islamophobia that can so easily afflict public discourse about Middle Eastern human bombing. Every-thing about human bombing is blamed on Islam. As University of Chicago political scientist Robert A. Pape notes in his *New York Times* OpEd of September 2003,

> Suicide terrorism has been on the rise around the world for two decades, but there is great confusion as to why. Since many such attacks – including, of course, those of Sept. 11, 2001 – have been perpetrated by Muslim terrorists professing religious motives, it might seem obvious that Islamic fundamentalism is the central cause. (Pape 2003)

Consequently, we also find a special term like 'Islamofascism' moving into wide circulation to capture this truth about the essential Islamic grounds of human bombing. This sort of language has been pro-moted by right-wing cultural critics like David Horowitz, Christopher Hitchens, and others eager to indict what they take to be anti-modern or fascistic trends among Muslims in the Middle East. They hope to label human bombers with this particularly noxious term, 'Islamofascist,' to emphasize their belief that the root cause of this sort of extremist political violence is Islam as a religion.

Yet, in doing so, Hitchens and company want to do more than indict a party of extremists within the Muslim community. Hitchens in particular seeks to smear both the entire Muslim religious tradition – and *religion* generally, as we have seen earlier – with the indelible stain of violence and fanaticism. (Hitchens 2007) As for Islam, Hitchens may at times defend these smears by pulling citations out of the Quran where violence is enjoined. These excerpts suffice to prove to him not only that the Islamofascists are solidly orthodox, but more broadly that Islam is, in general and at its roots, a fundamentally evil, bloodthirsty religion. Luckily for Hitchens, the now familiar hair-raising rhetoric issuing from Al Qaeda celebrating sacrifice, suicide, and death seems to give all the supporting evidence necessary to close the case for indicting Islam, either implicitly or not. Hitchens thus notes that equating Islam and fascism makes perfect sense:

> It is surely not an accident that both of them [Islam and fascism] stress suicidal tactics and sacrificial ends, just as both of them would obviously rather see the destruction of their own societies than any compromise with infidels or any dilution of the joys of absolute doctrinal orthodoxy. (Hitchens 2007)

Logically speaking, for Hitchens, since the human bombers in the Middle East are Muslims, and since Islam is a fundamentally violent religion, then the religion of Islam explains why these human bombers bomb. Case closed.

3. Dying to Make Too Little of Religion in 'Suicide' Bombing: Robert A. Pape

Or so one would think. Notable for reopening the case against a religious explanation of human bombing is University of Chicago political scientist Robert A. Pape. His book, *Dying to Win,* has been celebrated in social science circles and its arguments are repeated in OpEd pieces in major media outlets such as *The New York Times.* (Pape 2003) While Pape does not explicitly set out to take on those who would attribute human bombing explicitly to 'Islamofascism,' he tries to eliminate *religion* – whether Islam or not – from any kind of responsibility for human bombing in the Middle East. "The data show there is little connection between suicide terrorism and Islamic fundamentalism, or any religion for that matter ..." (Pape 2003) In support of this conclusion, Pape assembles a mighty batch of statistics from which he draws the conclusion that religion "is rarely the root cause [of human bombing]." At best, religion "is often used as a tool by terrorist organizations in recruiting and in other efforts of broader strategic objective." (Pape 2005, 38) At times, it seems as if Pape is addressing those who 'make too much of religion' and thus those who seek to blame something like 'Islamofascism' for human bombing. Dryly, Pape says that the "presumed connection [of human bombing in the Middle East] to Islamic fundamentalism is misleading." (Pape 2005, 38) Pape's book matters to us, then, because he represents a polar opposite to the likes of Hitchens by arguing that religion – Islamic or not – has no place at all in explaining an admittedly political phenomenon like human bombing in the Middle East. For my money, however, Pape makes 'too little' of the role of religion in political affairs, even as Hitchens and company make far too much.

To be completely fair to Pape, one would need to engage him on many levels, not least of which would be his use of statistical methodology. While I do not disparage quantitative methods, I cannot take them on here. In any event, the main point of bringing Pape into the discussion is merely to provide an example of someone who, in my view, 'makes too little' of religion in explaining human bombing in the Middle East. Pape actually contradicts himself, and in the process furthers my arguments for seeing religion as playing a serious role in human bombing in the Middle East. In this connection, there is at least one big problem with Pape's achievement. While it may be a good thing to rescue Islam from the libels of the Harrises and Hitchenses, I believe that it may come at too great a cost to our understanding. By denying that religion has anything substantial to do with human bombing in the Middle East, Pape impoverishes the phenomenon at hand. The force of my arguments throughout has been that if we look harder at 'religion,' 'power,' and 'politics,' if we interrogate those notions, then we can get new insights into the way things happen in the world. Pape does not look hard at any of these notions at all. In saying that religion is not a "root cause," for example, he seems to be hedging his bets against Islam's being some other kind of cause. Why cannot 'religion' be a significant 'cause' without being a "*root cause*"? And, what, pray tell, is a "*root* cause"? It is also odd that a social scientist should manage to approach religion in such an asocial way. Why does Pape seem to repeat all the errors of 'cognitivism' that Talal Asad (and I) rightly assail? (Asad 1993, ch. 1) Why, therefore, does Pape reduce the notion of religion to bare 'belief'? Why does he, therefore, cite only such cognitivist phenomena as "fundamentalism" and "religious indoctrination" in his understanding of the role of Islam in human bombing, as when he mentions only beliefs and doctrines? (Pape 2003; 2005, 16) Why, in short, is Pape's conception of religion so informed with commonplaces and clichés? Where is the lived-in, socio-cultural reality of religion – the emotional life, the daily routine practices and special ritualized occasions, the subtle shaping of time and space in response to the rhythms of a religious calendar, the disciplining and inscribing into the body by feast and famine, by exposure and covering, and so on? Where is the moral life of hate and love, of theft and gift, of sacrifice and self-interest? In vain will one find any of this amid the flurry of statistics that makes up so much of Pape's effort. I believe, however, that this is where precisely religion lodges – in the "embodied practices," and "networks of emotional connection," of which Talal Asad speaks. (Asad 1996, 1–15; 2005, 12) It is there, I am arguing in this chapter, where we can begin to see how religion plays in human bombing.

Incidentally, the more one reads Pape, the more it becomes clear how his avoidance of these embodied, social, and cultural dimensions of religion leaves him in a state of confusion about the relation of religion to human bombing. All the while touting how irrelevant religion is to an explanation of human bombing, at other points

Pape speaks of the "broad support within the national communities" that nourishes human bombers. (Pape 2005, 22) Would it surprise anyone if this "support" came from religious affiliation? And, if so, would belonging to such communities not in some way 'cause' the human bombing, say by establishing a context of meaning in which such acts acquire their authoritative power? Similarly, even as he dismisses the role of religion in explaining human bombing, Pape also says that if the religions of occupied and occupiers differ, "suicide terrorism" becomes "more likely." (Pape 2005, 22) But we must ask Pape why this should be the case, unless religion mattered in some material – causal – way. So, one must finally ask Pape where he comes down. Is religion a factor of significance in explaining human bombing in the Middle East, or is it not? Which Pape should we believe? Finally, if religion is a factor in explaining human bombing, in what ways precisely is it so?

4. No Religion in 'Suicide' Bombing: Talal Asad

Because of the uniqueness of his viewpoint, we must consider one other thinker determined to eliminate religion from an explanation of human bombing – Talal Asad. By denying the possibility of religious *agency* to the human bomber in the Middle East, Asad excludes religion from being a factor in explaining and understanding human bombing in the Middle East. Unlike Pape, who at least in principle accepts the possibility of people being *motivated* to become human bombers for religious reasons, Asad denies this possibility – at least in the context that concerns us here – the Middle East or Israel/Palestine. Asad does so from two 'angles' of attack.

Asad first seeks, generally, to vacate *moral responsibility* and *moral agency* from the world of Middle Eastern suicide bombers. Thus, Asad says that in the Middle East, we should see suicide bombers as simply triggered by facts on the ground. For Asad, *mutatis mutandis,* the human bomber might want to say something like "The Israelis made me do it!" It is, therefore, a mistake to think that human bombers "choose to justify their violence in terms of a discursive religious tradition." (Asad 2007, 45) They are not responsible for what happens, since they are fundamentally just resisters to an evil already in place. Victims of the agency of others, they have been "driven by an insupportable environment" to undertake their own deaths. (Asad 2007, 45) They see themselves, accordingly, as having been "struck dead by an external force," (Asad 2007, 50) as souls "struck by catastrophe." (Asad 2007, 49) They may seem like responsible actors, but in fact, they have simply engaged in "a spontaneous action when legal political means are blocked." (Asad 2007, 47) To attribute freedom of choice, or a sense of moral agency or responsibility, to them would be to misrepresent their situation. They are not agents, since they have no free choice. They are essentially passive victims whose apparent agency has its causes in the external oppression they suffer.

Having claimed that the human bombers in the Middle East are not true agents, Asad then feels that one cannot, secondly, understand them in terms of some kind of motive, especially an (inevitably libelous) Islamic – and thus, religious – one. To blame Islam for suicide bombing, as Hitchens, for example, enthusiastically does, not only passes over the injustice that spawns human bombers, but also indulges in a now all-too-familiar Islamophobia. "It is surely not an accident that both" Islam and fascism "stress suicidal tactics," Hitchens warns us. But, from Asad's point of view, such an ignorant indictment misplaces the moral and other responsibility for human bombing in Israel/Palestine, for instance. It is tantamount to "finding a culprit as well as the religious sources that feed his criminality." (Asad 2007, 45) Even if we could establish what was in the mind of a human bomber, and even if some religious motive were to be found there, it would be irrelevant to the causality of human bombing. For this reason, Asad argues that any attempt to see religious causes in human bombing in the Middle East must fail. There is a "larger story" to be told, and that "story does not begin by trying to explain a religious act," says Asad. (Asad 2007, 46) It begins (and ends, presumably) with a victimization narrative.

Given what we now know of those who 'make too much of religion' as a factor in human bombing in the Middle East, and those as well who, on the other side, 'make too little' of it, what proposal do I make in response? Following on what I have already argued in the foregoing chapters, it will be no surprise that I have serious issues with each of these positions on the relation of religion to the political act of human bombing in the Middle East. In response to Hitchens and company, I shall argue that he has made far too much of the responsibility of Islam for human bombing. While there may be some sort of relation between the two, it is not at all what Hitchens thinks. Here, I shall bring in the revamped notion of religion that I showcased in Chapter 2 to show how Islam might share some agency by providing a context of meaningfulness for human bombing. If Islam, or religion in general, shares some blame, Hitchens has not shown that he comprehends how this is might really be true. Hitchens imagines Islam as actively dictating the path a human bomber should follow from a list of beliefs or Quranic verses. Because strands of Islamic culture make it *understandable* how and why human bombers bomb is not at all the same thing as citing a *set of commands* to do so. Are we to blame the pope for the Oklahoma bombing by committed Christian terrorist Timothy McVeigh? Yet, we can understand some of McVeigh's worldview, and thus his motivation, from the meaning a particular strand of Christian theology gave to his act. What can be said of McVeigh can as well be said of the Ku Klux Klan. This would be true, for that matter, even more so for the Crusades, where explicit religious orders commanded their deeds! Medievalist Jean Flori, for example, has broken with the habit of looking euphemistically on the Crusades as 'pilgrimage,' even as "armed pilgrimage," and has argued that they were "holy wars," that is to say, the equivalent of jihads! (Flori 2001) Here, an active conception of the warrior martyr obliterates any possible differences between Christianity and Islam as to the active role of martyrs. (Cowdrey 1985, 46–56,

46; Flori 1991, 121–39) Guibert of Nogent's *The Deeds of God through the Franks* (1108) provides the text:

> No land on earth will ever see soldiers of such nobility fighting together. If you wish, I shall relate the story of every kingdom, speak of battles done everywhere; none of these will be able to equal either the nobility or the force of these men. They left their paternal lands, abandoned conjugal bonds, their children were unattractive to them, remaining at home was punishment for them; in every knight the desire for martyrdom burns. (Nogent 1997, 50–1)

Similarly, in the opposite case of Pape making 'far too little' of the role of Islam and religion, it is precisely these cultural elements that go into making meaning that need to be brought out in order to see how Islamic religion enters into the causality of human bombing. Finally, as for Asad, I shall attempt to reclaim a proper sense of agency, especially religious agency, in the causality of human bombing in the Middle East. This is not at all to gainsay Asad's well-taken point of the human bomber in Israel/Palestine being situated within the context of a resistance struggle. But, as I shall argue, it will be to enlarge the context beyond what Asad imagines. I seek to see the human bombers as they see themselves – as unusual sorts of politico-religious gifts, sacrifices, and martyrdoms, made comprehensible within an Islamic religious culture. There is, in short, such a thing as a jihadi or extremist Islam. It is fully Islamic, although a *fully* contestable Islam, and fully contestable as a religious phenomenon, as well. But, none of this means that the jihadis speak either for the bulk of the Islamic community or even a significant part of it. That is an empirical matter that could only be approached by social research.

5. How Religion Helps Explain Human Bombing

Accordingly, I shall show how an understanding of human bombers in the Middle East dictates that 'religion' cannot be eliminated from our analyses without fatal loss to our understanding. This as well will entail that I shall define 'religion' in a certain way, in part, consonant with my theoretical purposes of trying to understand human bombing in the Middle East. I am therefore not confined to commonsense or everyday definitions of 'religion,' and even less to the standard six clichés about the nature of religion, in order to offer an understanding of how religion is at play in human bombing in Israel/Palestine. Here, therefore, is a place where theoretical decision making will come to the fore, a place where one takes risks in offering a definition of religion deemed to be salient in the present situation. For me, religion must be taken seriously as a factor in many of the world's affairs, and I think human bombing in the Middle East is one of them. So, here is where one needs to ask the question of what 'religion' means in the situation in question. Here is where the old conventional understandings of religion and politics may not do. Here as well the clichés of the necessary goodness or badness of religion may not be assumed, but instead must become matters of fierce contest. Here is where the cliché of religion as belief gives way to a notion of religion in which practice, embodiment, emotion, and such may matter as much as, if not more than, belief – even including belief in God. Here also is where I have found it impossible to say whether politics is "using" religion or religion "using" politics. Rather, neither is "using" the other. Religion and politics are just doing what one should expect them to do, given a wiser understanding of both. Thus, here is where religion can be both public and a player in the game of political power, where the conventional clichéd assumptions about religion being this so-called 'spiritual' and internal reality do not always square with facts. Here then is where efforts both to eliminate religion from the equation and to see it only in the most conventionally cliché-ridden terms impoverish our understanding of human bombers in the Middle East.

Here, then, finally, is where the interrogations of 'power' and 'politics' I undertook in Chapters 3 and 4 show us how careful we need to be when we make assumptions about what words like 'power' and 'politics' should mean in connection with 'religion.'

Does the human bomber, for example, achieve their effects by means of *auctoritas* or *potestas,* or both? Empowered by a certain *auctoritas,* is the human bomber, therefore, someone who achieves – or could achieve – their aims by means of seizing command of a religio-moral scheme that in turn compels others to act in certain ways? Or, emboldened by their own *potestas,* do they mostly attain their ends by sheer exercise of political power, culminating in real violence – rather than the metaphorical kind of the expression "institutional violence"? Is the human bomber's power best understood as well in terms of Foucault's notion that power is diffused and generalized throughout the human world – that it is "co-extensive with the social body"? (Foucault 1977c, 134–45, 141) Or, is the 'power' of the human bomber better understood as being focused on the State, including the nation as an "imagined community," a nation-state in becoming? And then, is Foucault's idea of power as "a dynamic energy that infuses a social system" the best tool for prying open the mysteries of human bombing? (Chidester 1988, 8) Or, contrary to Foucault's wishes, as I shall argue, must reference to the State and nation always be a part of our talk about power used in the sense of *potestas* – power politics? Likewise, when it comes to the consequences of interrogating 'politics' in cases like human bombing, I believe that we can best do so with the rich notions of religion and politics that our interrogations have produced over the previous chapters.

6. Human Bombing Is "Catastrophe," but also a "Triumph" of "Secular Immortality"

Let me begin a detailed reply to the eliminationist arguments first. A good reason for keeping religion in mind when we try to understand human bombers – at the very least, 'religion' in the everyday sense as including Islam – is their own words. It will become rapidly clear that these will neither sustain Asad's picture of irresponsibility and victimhood, nor will they make it easy for Pape to write off religion entirely. What, then, is the nature of the positive vision of agency and responsibility informing human bombing – now unexpectedly reappearing in religious guise in talk of sacrifice, gift, immortality, and triumph in the face of death?

With the issue of agency foremost in mind, let's begin exploring just what human bombing in the Middle East seems to be. If agents they are, and not just the passive victims of catastrophe Asad makes them out to be, what would be a prime candidate for understanding the agency of suicide bombers? Unremarkably, if we go by what the human bombers themselves say, 'jihad' must top the list. The idea that human bombers see themselves as fighting jihadis certainly overshadows the view that "human bombers" should naturally be called "suicides." Self-inflicted death is one thing. But self-inflicted death as a weapon in a struggle is something else entirely. In Muslim terms, absent the context of struggle, and even with conscious religious intent added in, the mere fact of self-inflicted death can never guarantee one's place in Paradise. It is the fact of a struggle for justice or to protect Islam that prevents, at least *prima facie,* out-and-out condemnation for human bombing.

What, at least, is one part of the vision of what "human bombings" in Israel/Palestine mean to the actors themselves? Answering directly, one can say without reservation that whatever else they may be, these bombings are undeniably about killing Jews, Israelis, Palestinian collaborators, and, well beyond ending an occupation, of eliminating Israel itself. Human bombers are about making a violent projection of *potestas.* (Significantly, they are very much not about some concerted campaign of non-violent resistance.) The declarations of Hamas and other organizations involved in them have made this abundantly clear. Hamas, for example, focuses on the suffering caused to the enemy by the "human bombers" rather than "extolling their own suffering." In the minds of the human bombers themselves, they not only embrace responsibility, but assert it with vigor. The Charter of Hamas, for example, says a great deal about eliminating Israel and jihad. (Israeli 1997, 96–112, 96) Hizballah likewise demands that the deaths of their "human bombers" be justified by the suffering of the number of casualties inflicted on the enemy. (Israeli 2002, 23–40, 23) These examples, informed as they are by the active discourse of jihad, should also counsel caution about speaking too simply of other conceptions of human bombing, such as those (Talal Asad's in fact, as we will see) that rob the human bombers of agency and responsibility for their acts. They themselves vociferously claim the human bombings to be brave, heroic, martyring deeds. Similarly, the fact of the salience of jihad should give second thoughts, as well, to those who might see human bombings (as I do myself) in terms of their *auctoritas,* rather than sheer *potestas.* In this way, the jihadist element of human bombing serves as a fine example of what Brian S. Turner and Frédéric Volpi observe as "the profusion of arbitrary authority structures that seek forcefully to impose their views as authoritative." (Volpi & Turner 2007, 1–19, 11) I shall argue that the human bombers ought accordingly to be seen as projecting *auctoritas* in their roles as sacrifices. Sacrifices, unlike jihads, are not typically directed *against* the interests of another, but are, by contrast, peculiar kinds of 'gifts' *offered* to or for others. It is as givers of significant 'gifts' that human bombers get their *auctoritas* or authority. It is how they become 'heroes' for the Palestinian resistance.

To be sure, in the minds of human bombers, jihad in Israel/ Palestine, as Asad claims, is an act done within the context of *reaction* to the military reality of Israel. But this does not settle much, since there is no referee to declare who 'threw the first punch' – who is objectively *reacting* to whom. Was the First Crusade 'aggression' (and the Crusaders, therefore, moral 'agents') or was the First Crusade only a reaction to the Muslim conquest and occupation of previously Christian lands? It is a commonplace that in a conflict each side will blame the other for 'starting it.' Aren't Israeli military operations routinely seen by Israelis as *reactions* to rocket attacks, or to the overall military threat of being encircled by vast numbers of hostile Arabs? The mere citation of grievances never settles anything. For every Palestinian grievance, one can be sure, whether well founded or not, there will be as many Israeli ones.

Yes, the perceived indignities of military occupation and the expansion of Israeli colonies on Arab land can nevertheless inspire "rage." (Asad 2007, 47) Fighters may also calculate – of course, never wrongly in the minds of those like Asad – that since they experience "injustice," "spontaneous action" in the form of violence is the only alternative remaining to them. (Asad 2007, 47) Forget for a moment that such outbursts of violence by the Palestinians may only play into the hands of the occupation, as even some Palestinians have argued. The point to be made here is that there is nothing new in Asad's attempt to reconstruct the emotional context that feeds the Palestinian resistance – even if Asad imagines that there is. Any partner in a struggle will justify themselves by claiming to act in self-defense. But what is critical is that these justifications are made with their own *religious arguments* – which Asad conveniently discounts, although he constantly scolds others for ignoring the 'native point of view.' (Asad 2007, 44) If one is going to insist on making the announced perspectives of the human bombers pertinent to our understanding of their acts, then we cannot just choose those perspectives that reinforce our own political agenda, as Asad demonstrably does. We need to face the complicating fact that human bombing in the Middle East is a complex and doubtless overdetermined thing, merging religion and politics.

Thus, if we can get past these hopeless attempts to shift moral responsibility to the other party, at the end of the day we need to restore a proper sense of agency, responsibility, and such to the human bombers. This is not to assign some sort of mythical 100 percent responsibility to the human bombers, any more than we can to the acts of any person in real life. But we do need to reclaim a proper sense of agency over against Asad's determination to vacate agency – and, in particular *religious agency* – from the world of suicide bombers. To forsake any sense of agency in the minds of human bombers is, at the very least, to forsake working "through the concepts the people concerned actually use." (Asad 2007, 44)

Oddly enough, Asad may turn out to have made one of the better arguments against his own denial of *religious agency* to the human bombers. At a certain juncture in his argument, even Asad has to admit that if the human bombers see themselves passively – as "struck by catastrophe" – they also see themselves in what looks for all the world in religious terms as actors. Such a death, for instance, "constitutes a triumph" (Asad 2007, 49), and one, as well, that achieves a "secular immortality." (Asad 2007, 47, 49) If indeed this is so, are we not compelled to press for clarity about what the vision of such a "triumph" is? What positive content and methods fund such a victory? Is there, for example, a territory in which "triumph" is enjoyed? Is there some sort of political entity in which this "triumph" is realized? Where, as well, do those having achieved their alleged "immortality" dwell? Given that such a discourse of *religious agency* flies in the face of the secular victim narrative that Asad announces, there is every reason why we ought not to expect answers to such questions from Asad.

Against the incoherence, then, of Asad's view, I am pressed to pick up the lead provided by the suicide bombers themselves in talking of 'triumph' and 'immortality.' My main argument is that another part of the agency of human bombers consists in their thinking of themselves as gifts to the *umma,* as *religious* sacrifices. Again, this is not to deny external forces acting upon the human bombers, their having been "driven by an insupportable environment." (Asad 2007, 45) Despite Asad's attempts to paint the suicide bomber in passive terms – as souls "struck by catastrophe" (Asad 2007, 49) – I do not think the evidence of the words of suicide bombers will sustain such a picture of pathetic victimhood, when so much is said about their being gifts and sacrifices (as well as jihadis, of course). Indeed, the ordinary usage of the Arabic for "gift" (*hadiyya*) connects it closely to the most common words for sacrifice, proper, "*adha*" and "*qurban.*" Semantically, *hadiyya* also means sacrifice and offering, even though this usage is not widespread, doubtless because of the dominance of other terms for sacrifice, namely, *adha* and *qurban.* Nonetheless, despite its lack of popular currency, the close relation of *haddiya* and *adha/qurban* allows us to link the two as both gift and sacrifice. (Ali 2008, pers. comm.)

7. Human Bombing = Jihad + Sacrifice

In response to those who take jihad – as either active or passive – as the only way to see human bombing, we are obliged to register contrary facts. Other salient conceptions of human bombing emerge from the mouths of the human bombers themselves. In their eyes, they have dual religious roles: they are holy warriors fighting in jihad, but they are also martyrs and sacrifices. Here, I do not speak of sacrifice as some kind of moral attitude or state of mind as typically assumed by the liberal religious-thinking West. Recall from our interrogation of 'religion' how Liberal Protestant thinkers queried the very religiousness of embodied forms of religion, like sacrifice. A prominent theologian of the late nineteenth century called sacrifice an example of "religious materialism." As such, any so-called religion giving central place to ritual observance and practices was "always more or less superstitious" – that is to say, not really religion at all. (Réville 1874, 138–56, 151) This refusal of the embodied quality of religion was in effect an effort at spiritualization. Here, for these Liberal Protestant theologians, if sacrifice were to be entertained, it had to be viewed from a "more elevated moral and religious sense" (Réville 1874, 138–56, 154) – as a "yearning of the believer for abiding communion with" God. (Tiele 1898, 149) By contrast, the sacrifice of the human bombers is fully, if gruesomely embodied, so much so that it gives rise to shocking bloody imagery. Recently, one potential human bomber delighted in the prospect that upon explosion, pieces of his flesh would be scattered out over a wide area of enemy territory, some even clinging to the bodies of the foe. (Lawrence 2005) Thus, reporting on the views of potential women human bombers after 9/11, Sandra Jordan reports in London's *New Statesman* how they see themselves in terms both of jihad and sacrifice alike:

> "We know what Palestine needs from us," said Reham. "Jihad. If Usama had chosen differently, he would have been living for himself, but failing Palestine. Everyone should choose sacrifice until we

restore our rights. Israelis are occupying our land and we have to get rid of it. Jihad is the only way." (Jordan 2002)

Similarly, if we take Osama bin Laden at his word, the 9/11 hijackers were similarly 'sacrifices', as well as 'martyrs.' Said bin Laden, "The 19 brothers who sacrificed their lives in the sake of God were rewarded by this victory that we rejoice today." In another place, bin Laden celebrated "Hani Hanjour from Al-Ta'if, the destroyer of the centre of the US defence, the Pentagon. Clear purity and a splendid sacrifice. We beseech God to accept him as a martyr." (bin Laden 2001) Insofar, then, as the human bombers reflect *agency,* they see their actions mixing both jihad *and* sacrifice. And, just to make matters more complex, they throw in martyrdom as well. Even as these three notions can – and ought to – be teased apart for the sake of simplicity, the complexity of their interdependence remains undeniable too.

What then becomes clear from these and many other assertions of the centrality of sacrifice in the radical Muslim or Islamist point of view about suicide bombings is that in the minds of Hamas, Al Qaeda, and others, such operations are equally well named 'sacrifice bombings,' 'martyrdom operations,' or something similar. In this light, the term 'suicide bombing' turns out to be a particularly unhelpful pejorative. At the very least, not losing sight of the fact that 'jihad' retains its power, I shall try to show how multivalent the discourse about "human bombers" is. Religious notions like 'sacrifice' are one of the most prominent 'voices' making up the chorus. My argument is thus that even if we grant jihad its rightful place at the conceptual high-table of "human bombings," in order more fully to understand even some jihadist aspects of "human bombings," we may have to adopt something even more of the viewpoint of an Islam that repeats again and again that human bombers are religious in the sense of being sacrifices. I am urging us, then, to pay more attention to the nuances, qualifications, and inner contradictions of the standard interpretation of "human bombings" as jihad pure and simple might suggest that we do. Jihad, I think, is only part of the story of the "human bombers," and only part of the way their agency is a religious one as much as it is political.

I thus believe that such language gives us warrant to delve more deeply into the profundities of an even more Islamic frame of reference for understanding the motives of so-called suicide bombers. That Islamic frame of reference for the "human bombings" is, I believe, more than just jihad, it is sacrifice. The Islamic character of human bombing lies at deeper levels than meets the everyday eye. In Israel/Palestine, while one element of the agency of these self-inflicted deaths is to attack others outright in jihad, then another, and simultaneous, one is to create a Palestinian political entity by making a sacrificial offering to Allah and the *umma*. "Human bombers" aim to kill Jews, but as agents they also are embedded in their families and communities, and in a world encompassed by a supreme being that has a political teleology of its own well in excess of killing Jews or any other perceived enemies. The meaning of the actions of the "human bombers" derives at least in part from the web of both human and divine relationships in which they seem themselves living, now and as they imagine their extended families and people living in the future. There is more to "human bombers" than jihad, and certainly more than suicide. There is, as I shall now argue, sacrifice. Thus, in a video to be shown on or near Christmas Day 2001, on Al Jazeera, bin Laden taunted the United States for its hypocrisy in the face of the 9/11 attacks, here stressing that the hijackers were a mere "nineteen post-secondary students" who made the ultimate sacrificial gift of their own lives:

> Every day, from east to West, our umma of 1200 million Muslims is being slaughtered, in Palestine, in Iraq, Somalia, Western Sudan, Kashmiri, the Philippines, Bosnia, Chechnya, and Assam. We do not hear their voices, yet *as soon as the victim rises up and offers himself on behalf of his religion,* people are outraged. 1200 million Muslims are being slaughtered without anyone even knowing, but if anyone comes to their defense, those people just repeat whatever the tyrants want them to say. (My emphasis; Lawrence 2005, 153)

In the same address, bin Laden once more underlines that the 9/11 attacks – an act of jihad – were also a total sacrificial gift, here made for the sake of Islam: "these *[the 9/11 attackers] are the people who have given up everything* for the sake of 'There is no god but God' …" (My emphasis; Lawrence 2005, 154)

So pervasive is the language of sacrifice that Al Qa'eda defector "Max" even spoke of devotion to Osama bin Laden in sacrificial terms. Referring to the companions of bin Laden, "Max" could say the following:

> Yeah, you know, each of them wanted to sacrifice for Usama bin Laden. They want to spend their money and their – everything – to sacrifice themselves for bin Laden. There was, you know, anyone that bin Laden asked them to do – to kill themselves, to sacrifice themselves for bin Laden. He won't say no. There are a thousand people; they want to sacrifice themselves for bin Laden. (Max)

The words of human bombers and those connected to them tell us that it is not that difficult to know what motives are at play, simply because "the actor dies in the event." They are as "retrievable" as are the motives of many a common suicide, even though I am arguing that these are anything but common suicides. (Asad 2007, 45) Secondly, if we also follow the perfectly reasonable rule that "to talk of religious subjectivities, one must work through the concepts of the people concerned," then *both* 'jihad' and 'sacrifice' demonstrably play roles in human bombing. (Asad 2007, 44) At the very least, these two ways of thinking about human bombings will need to be untangled.

Having treated 'jihad' already as a projection of power in the sense of *potestas,* I am claiming that the significance of the religious or sacrificial discourse in human bombing is its projection of another sense of power entirely – namely *auctoritas.* Indeed, if we follow Dumont's suggestion, speaking of 'power' here *without qualification* only perpetuates one of Orwell's "bad habits" of thinking by speaking 'badly.' Sacrifice is not about killing the *enemy;* there is no *potestas* in it for *enemies.* In fact, in some cases, the *potestas* of the jihadi act of self-immolation in human bombing is, in a way, incidental to the self-sacrifical act. Even some human bombers who fail to kill anyone but themselves still retain as much *auctoritas* as those who succeed in projecting jihadi *potestas* by killing the enemy. *That* is the quality I seek to capture. Even when an attack sometimes fails, the bomber will detonate their charges anyway. One must assume that foremost in the minds of some bombers is the *sacrificial* intention – the aim to give up one's life for the intended goal – to sacrifice – even when no practical benefit in terms of an attack obtains. More obviously, human bombing as sacrifice has emphasized the self of *self*-sacrifice, and thus if it is about killing, it is about killing oneself. Hence the term 'suicide bomber' has had a wide, but misleading, currency. As we will see, on the contrary, human bombing as sacrifice is the projection of an *auctoritas* that has nothing essentially to do with warring against an enemy, or even about killing an enemy. It is an act projecting an *auctoritas* that creates something by making something sacred. It is the *auctoritas* that enhances a community and that depends solely upon being embraced by it. To secure what may be this disturbing, indeed, to some, morally offensive interpretation of human bombing, I need to say a few words about suicide and its relation to sacrifice.

8. Sacrifice or Suicide?

When words like 'sacrifice' or 'suicide' enter conversations, it is pretty obvious that they are not neutral designations, but 'loaded' value words. Calling a death 'suicidal' not only *describes* how a person died, but weighs it down with a hefty moral or social judgment. Similarly, referring to a death as 'sacrificial' or as 'martyrdom' lifts it to lofty levels of religious transcendence. Sacrificial deaths are supposed to be noble, high above the profane calculation of individual cost–benefit analysis. Sacrifice is supposed to be about a so-called 'higher' good, whether that be of a nation or some transnational or transcendent reference, like a religion. From such heights, sacrifice

164

also lays claim to a certain *auctoritas* – a certain moral potency that influences how others act in response to it. The response of a nation to the 'sacrificial' deaths of its soldiers is often to renew the effort for which they died. Sacrifice can then be said to become the seat of an *auctoritas* from which influence can be exerted. This, as we will see, sets it apart from the way that the *potestas* of jihad gets things done. The sacrifices of non-violent demonstrators made of themselves in Gandhi's India or Martin Luther King, Jr.'s by offering up their bodies to the blows of their oppressors may have seemed foolish from the point of view of sheer power – *potestas*. But their example served to create decisive moral pressure and authority – *auctoritas* – in behalf of their respective causes.

This insight informs the classic treatment of suicide and sacrifice of the French sociologist Émile Durkheim. He puzzled over how to conceive what he called "altruistic suicide" – cases of individuals giving up their lives for others, as say in a war where soldiers die to save their comrades. Durkheim's problems arose because it could not be explained why – in strictly numerical material and utilitarian terms – acts of self-destruction did not result in society destroying itself too. In material terms, how could one 'add' to the social whole, so to speak, by 'subtracting' its own constituent human members – and 'subtracting' them voluntarily? Yet, certain acts of self-destruction, such as 'altruistic suicide,' functioned for social flourishing. Was it, then, a misnomer to call such deeds 'suicides' at all, since this implied kinship with precisely those malignant suicidal deaths that did not at all function for social flourishing? Would it not be better to call them something else – something signaling that these altruistic 'suicidal' (sic) deaths partook of another kind of causality than a material one? Durkheim's great ambition was precisely to make such a case for social, ideal, or moral causality. These forms of causality were nonetheless 'natural,' like material causality. (Pickering 1984, 210) He was not talking about miracles or supernatural forces, like grace. Social forces just operated at another "level," reflecting another sort of reality from that of brute matter. (Pickering 1984, 278)

In exploring social causes, Durkheim said that they had two aspects – a negative one as "social constraints" and a positive one as "dynamogenic forces." The "paradigm sense" of 'constraints' was "the exercise of authority, backed by sanctions, to get individuals to conform to rules." These are what I, following Dumont, have been calling *auctoritas*. The *auctoritas* of social control is what we all experience and recognize as the 'power' – the authority – of collective opinion, social pressure, conformity, conventional wisdom, entrenched beliefs, 'commonsense,' trends, fashions, fads, and such. On the positive side, for Durkheim, social "forces" could also be inspiring and dynamic spurs to action – the "causal factors inducing men" among other things to "break the rules." (Lukes 1972, 13) We will recall again that Durkheim identified these "dynamogenic forces" with the presence of religion. It is the principal agent of the 'power' of *auctoritas* and, in effect, "produces social energy" that spurs social "activity and change." (Pickering 1984, 214)

This nexus of *auctoritas,* social causality, dynamogenic forces, and religion seems precisely why Durkheim preferred to think about so-called 'altruistic suicides' as 'sacrifices' instead. They were really only 'suicides' in the superficial sense of a self-inflicted death. In all other respects, they called for a name reflecting their felt role in social flourishing. But Durkheim made little or no progress on conceiving how this 'subtraction' of a member from society could actually 'add' to it. That task was left to one of his more talented co-workers, Maurice Halbwachs. In his *The Causes of Suicide* (1930), Halbwachs revisited the question of the relation of suicide to sacrifice. He argued that whether something was to be called a 'sacrifice' rather than a 'suicide' depended upon the viewpoint of their respective societies of reference. "Society claims sacrifice as its own proper work," accomplished "within the bosom of the community, where all the spiritual forces converge," says Halbwachs. Society thus "presides" over sacrifice; it "organizes" it and "takes responsibility for it." By contrast, society "repudiates" suicide. I am suggesting that Halbwachs felt that societies decided to conceive certain self-inflicted deaths as 'sacrifice' rather than 'suicide' because they felt that these 'sacrifices' projected the 'power' of their *auctoritas* – the positive, dynamogenic, authorizing, inspiring, energizing forces that fed the formation or survival of a society. Thus, the 'subtraction' of a member of a society by self-inflicted death – sacrifice – can actually constitute 'addition' to the flourishing of that society because a death conceived as a 'sacrifice' can authorize, inspire, stimulate, or, critically, put others under an obligation to make greater efforts for the sake of that society's flourishing.

In Israel/Palestine, the Israeli writer Avishai Margalit confirms Halbwachs' insight. Margalit notes that while human bombers are motivated by *potestas* – by vengeance marked by a strong desire for "spectacular revenge," something else is afoot. These acts of human bombing are also profoundly social acts in Halbwachs' sense, since their success relies upon communal recognition and subsequent ritual celebration by the community from which the bomber comes. Social prestige accrues to the bombers to the extent that everyone knows their names – especially "small children." Human bombers are raised above the profane everyday into the realm of heroes – achieving what Asad noted as a "secular immortality." (Asad 2007, 47, 49) From this religio-moral high ground, they inspire and stimulate society to flourish. Other observers of human bombing in the Middle East record that these bombings are done with the expressed purpose of 'adding' to the social whole – in Islamic parlance, so that the "entire Islamic umma is rescued." (Margalit 2003, 36–9, 38.) Here, as Halbwachs' theory would pre-dict, Palestinian society is "claiming sacrifice as its own proper work," as something to be cherished by it "within the bosom of the community," and consequently as something Palestinian society grants *auctoritas* since it "takes responsibility for it." Understood by their agents and the societies to which they belong as 'sacrifices,' the self-inflicted deaths of the human bombers in the Middle East are suffused with a conviction that they actually 'add' to social flourishing, even though from material calculation, they seem to be 'subtracting' members from society. Although Palestinians who embrace these deaths "within the bosom of the community" may experience them as "catastrophe," we can understand why they also see them as "a triumph" because of the dynamogenic force they inject into society. (Asad 2007, 49)

9. But Do *Any* Muslims Really Think Human Bombers Are 'Sacrifices'?

Now, before moving on to deepen my religious reading of human bombing in the Middle East, I shall need briefly to address a critic of any religious, even less so Islamic, reading of human bombing in the Middle East. Here, we need to return to Talal Asad, who claims that "none of the criteria" that one might derive from "the Islamic tradition" (now curiously essentialized by Asad) justifies referring to suicide bombers as "sacrifices." (Asad 2007, 43–4)

Unfortunately for Asad, Muslim authoritative voices in today's world say otherwise. Common words for sacrifice among Middle Eastern Muslims are *qurban* and *adha*. Indeed, *adha* and *qurban* are synonymously used for one another in the Middle East by Muslims. Somewhat more salient than *qurban* is *adha*. The root meaning of *adha* comes from the word *dhaha,* which carries the meanings "to appear,""to sacrifice,""to offer up," and so on. *Adha* thus carries the meaning of actualizing one's commitment to Allah in material, tangible form, visible in the eyes of Allah. As far as speaking of human bombers as "sacrifices" in the sense of *adha* is concerned, the term can be applied to sacrificing oneself – a giving-up of one's life – as well as the more moderate notion of sacrifice as a giving-of – offering up one's property, for instance. One of the ways, then, in which human bombers see themselves is by interpreting their self-inflicted deaths as cases of *adha.* (Ali 2008, pers. comm.)

Another word, *udhiyya,* refers to the blood sacrifice at the Hajj ceremony to commemorate the Ibrahim/Abraham–Ishmael/Isaac sacrifice story. But it also means the gift for those celebrating the Hajj feast, but who do not participate in the Hajj itself. Incidentally, the word *udhiyya* shares the same root with the word for "gift" – *haddiyya*. *Haddiyya* literally denotes the meaning of gift for those who actually do perform the Hajj. The upshot of this little discursus into Arabic etymology is simply to show how an elaborate network of related ideas link the many terms for 'sacrifice' – *adha*, *qurban* and *udhiyya* – with the notion of "gift" – *haddiya*. The salience of this linking of gift and sacrifice will become clear as we conclude this chapter by showing how the human bombers see themselves *both* as sacrifices and as gifts – from a Muslim point of view. In saying this, I thus reaffirm the main point of this chapter that the human bombings in the Middle East are complexes of *both* politics and religion, in the sense of being projections of both *potestas* and *auctoritas*. Little more is necessary to refute Asad than to cite current literature about human bombers in the Muslim media.

Although I would not go so far as to essentialize Islam as Asad has done, there is a rough and ready way one can speak of a kind of consensus among Muslims about sacrifice, and certainly about human sacrifice. A traditional model that features Ibrahim/Abraham and his attempted sacrifice of Ishmael /Isaac does exist, and has been normative over a long period of time. Because, as we will see, the story resists easy univocal interpretations, it is all the more puzzling why Asad, for example, should express such confidence in knowing what it implies about sacrifice. As already noted, one of the common words for sacrifice here is *adha*. "Adha" is the name of the great feast celebrating the end of Ramadan, the "Eid al adha," and thus the liberation of Ishmael from his intended sacrifice by Ibrahim/Abraham. Thus, Sheik Yaseen, founder of Hamas, who abjures Muslims in the following language: "Remember our Eid is not an Eid of victory. It is the Eid of sacrifice (adha)." (Yaseen) Here, Yaseen refers, of course, to the Eid al-Adha, that feast celebrating the end of the Hajj.

The roots of Muslim conceptions of sacrifice as *adha* then point us toward ritual and scriptural contexts ultimately linked with Ibrahim/Abraham and the attempted sacrifice of Ishmael/Isaac. With Ibrahim/Abraham as a paradigm, Muslims inform their readiness to give of themselves for Allah, and routinely thus practice charitable giving, known as *zakat,* that counts as one of the five pillars of Islam. As well, Muslims think about civic sacrifice by thinking with ritual sacrifice; they also think about special civic sacrifices, as in a military operation, in jihad, by thinking with 'adha' or the sacrifice of Ishmael/Isaac, and so on. Some interpreters, therefore, claim that both father and son accept the command to sacrifice Ishmael literally and earnestly:

> People today may see themselves as individuals and that they are independent, that they have no responsibility to anybody, that the ahkam sharia does not apply to them, they don't care about what the Muslim Ummah is facing, they say that Islam only applies to individuals in their houses and should have no effect in life.
> Did Ibrahim (as) carry this idea that he is independent, that he is an 'individual' who does not have to take the orders of anybody. Was he selfish? Did Ismael take his own benefit rather than what Allah had commanded? Did Ibrahim (as) disobey the command of Allah to sacrifice his son? On the basis that he was an individual and that was against his benefit? (Anon. 1998)

Another commentator reinforces the place of sacrificial metaphors drawn from the story of Ibrahim/Abraham and Ishmael/Isaac in thinking about jihad. The duty of Muslims is to grasp the "Significance of Eid":

> These are the signs of our Ismail's. Let us search for them in ourselves (swt) and let us slaughter them to move towards Allah (swt) to remove the real knife from the throat of oppressed Muslims from Bosnia to Kashmir, from Somalia to Palestine. Let us revolt against the heartless worshipers that we have become. Remember our Eid is not an Eid of victory. It is the Eid of sacrifice (adha). (Anon. n.d. a)

But thinking about civic sacrifice based on a story from an ancient scripture is frequently fraught with problems of interpretation. The story of Ibrahim/Abraham's attempted sacrifice of

Ishmael/Isaac is no exception. Closest to the prevailing spirit of the moderate traditional reading of the Ibrahim/Abraham story are those we might call today's Muslim humanists. Perhaps reacting to the extreme sacrificial view of Hamas and others, these Muslim humanists seem intent upon striking a balance regarding sacrifice for the community over against a deep reverence for individual human life:

> How is a wall built? How do the individual blocks 'join ranks' to turn into a solid and impregnable wall? As a wall is composed of many building blocks, so must our communities be built upon the strengths of individuals like yourself ...
>
> When the wall is seen from a distance, the blocks may look indistinguishable due to their uniformity, but like human beings, each retains its inner individuality. No one is required to sacrifice this ... (Anon. n.d. d)

The humanists reinforce their reverence for the individual by employing a clever if, as we will see, a contorted, interpretive stratagem. Here, they take the Quran at its word to feature how the text itself offers an excuse for both Abraham and Allah to avoid responsibility for the possible slaying of Ishmael. The device consists in noting that the Quran literally says that Abraham arrived at the idea of sacrificing Ishmael in a dream: "O my son," says Abraham, "I have seen in a dream that I should sacrifice you." In the view of the humanists, this gives Abraham an 'out' since Allah might well not have commanded him to sacrifice Ishmael in reality. There never really was any danger of anyone understanding the dream's command as earnest and straightforward. While Abraham does lead Ishmael up to the sacrificial mount, by the device of invoking the 'dream' Allah is excused of ordering the sacrifice of Ishmael. 'I did no such thing old chap! You just dreamt it!' This nicely protects the belief that Allah cherishes the sacredness of every human being, even if it leaves us to wonder about why Abraham went through the motions of initiating sacrifice. Nevertheless, the device serves its purpose for Muslim humanists to find a way out of what looks like a direct command to immolate a human being.

Another article unambiguously entitled, "God never Ordered Abraham to Sacrifice His Son," takes up the same line, conceivably as well in opposition to the extreme view. Thus, the author explains that "Traditional Muslim Scholars have been teaching the Muslims that God inspired Abraham to sacrifice his son Ismail by slaughtering him with a knife. This is completely against what the Quran states." Among the arguments marshaled are these – all interestingly based on *literal* quotations from the Quran:

> The Quran never said that God told Abraham to kill (sacrifice) his son. Instead, the Quran teaches us that Abraham had a dream in which he saw himself slaughtering his son. Abraham believed the dream and thought that the dream was from God (The Quran never said the dream was from God). The choice of the wording in the Quran is crucial. No word was chosen by accident or out of control. Every word and expression was deliberately chosen by God.

Reasoning further, the same document argues that the failure of the Quran to record that God made such a demand upon Ibrahim/Abraham, moreover, fits with the claim that "Islam never advocated human sacrifice." For this reason, "God would not contradict Himself and order Abraham to commit what he prohibited even as a test." Denying even more deeply the implications of those who would accuse Islam of preaching that Ibrahim/Abraham was commanded by Allah to sacrifice Ishmael/Isaac, the same document tells us that "No where in the Quran does God say that it was God who told Abraham to sacrifice his son." And, undercutting that view even more, the document continues, "No where in the Quran does God say He gave Abraham that dream." (Anon. n.d. b)

In light of Asad's refusal to see anything of religion in the politics of human bombing, it would be well, then, to remind readers of the rise of the modern militant deviations from the traditional Abrahamic model. It is precisely these Muslims who sponsor human bombing, and they do it by appealing to *authority* deriving from religious models, precedents, scriptural passages, and such. Competition over such authority within Islam itself has thus become especially fierce, demanding the most powerful means of asserting it. Brian S. Turner and Frédéric Volpi bring out how the tensions in this changing and competitive world of Islamic authority tend to express themselves in acts of public violence. "But discourse, particularly discourses about religion and its inescapable authority over human life, do not occur in a vacuum; ultimately, these discourses have to be re-embodied and authority displayed in the public space (most vividly through violence)." This is so, not because Muslims or Islam is, by (historical) nature, prone to violence, but because the overarching structures of authority may no longer embrace a sufficient number of Muslims to insure stability across a whole spectrum of human thought and action:

> The competitive claim to legitimacy and authority … has an inflationary impact on the claims to superiority. To demonstrate my orthodoxy against your claims, I must increase the stakes, and … demonstrate that my interpretation of the law is more comprehensive, more demanding, more exacting and more all-embracing. (Volpi & Turner 2007, 1–19, 11)

Thus, even when some of these sponsors of human bombing shy away from the model of Ibrahim/Abraham precisely because of the textual ambiguity of the attempted sacrifice of Ishmael/Isaac, religious authorizations are not abandoned. They simply shift according to the new standards set by different groups. "What we obtain," in cases of novel interpretation, "is not a straightforward privatization of knowledge and authority," claim Brian S. Turner and Frédéric Volpi, "but rather a multiplication of authorities on the sacred text in what remains a two-tiered global communal order." (Volpi & Turner 2007, 1–19, 12) One such 'multiplication' affects readings of our Ibrahim/Abraham story. Thus, if Ibrahim/Abraham is either too ambiguous and contested a paradigm, or if it does not fit the particular needs to lay claim to a sufficient degree of authority for what one wants to do, perhaps shifting to scriptural evidence featuring Muhammad will? Perhaps scriptural passages featuring the Prophet might provide stronger legitimation for human bombing?

Whether or not appealing to Muhammad really does offer this stronger kind of legitimation, the militants believe that such new meaning structures can be substituted for older ones. They cast the Prophet as the chief exemplar of both self-sacrificial death and self-sacrifice ("tad'hia") linked essentially with jihad. As one militant Islamic scholar, Malik ibn Anas, *Ahahith al-Jami' al 'Saghir* in *Qira'a a fi, Fiqh al-Shahada,* pointed to:

> the famous Hadith, where the Prophet undertook to die for Allah, to come back to life and then die once again. This means that there was no bigger goal in the Prophet's own existence than to die for Allah, and repeatedly so. (Israeli 2002, 23–40, 4 n. 17)

Self-sacrifice thus becomes integral to situations where jihad is enjoined, despite Asad's resistance to such a characterization of human bombers. This sort of self-immolating jihad has moreover been proposed as "the standard behavior of all Muslims who seek battle at the highest level of risk." (Israeli 2002, 23–40, 4 n. 17)

From these hermeneutic maneuvers alone, we can conclude that there are such Muslims whom one might reasonably call 'extreme jihadis' and the like. Whatever the precise term used to name them, at least *these* Muslims represent an "Islamic tradition" that conceives of human bombers as sacrifices. Despite what those like Asad may want us to believe, therefore, there are, on the face of it at least, Muslim *agents* of human bombing and self-immolation, who understand and authorize their deeds consciously in terms of a particular tradition of Islamic religion. While they recognize their position in a conflict with others, they do not see themselves as determined by these conditions, but as projecting both the *potestas* of jihad and the *auctoritas* of sacrifice for the sake of some sort of positive end, whether that be the *umma* or, as I shall argue shortly, the nation-state, or "imagined community" of Palestine.

10. Sacrifice Makes Authority

I trust I have persuaded readers that as far as human bombers in the Middle East are concerned, some thinkers, Asad and Pape, for example, 'make too little of religion,' and Hitchens, Horowitz, and company 'make far too much' of it. I have argued, instead, that a significant part of the 'power' of suicide bombing comes from its being religious, but not in the ways either of these sets of thinkers understands. The trick is to see how and where religion does matter to human bombing in the Middle East. I am arguing that religion, Islam included, is implicated in human bombings, but mostly because religions like Islam and others create social worlds of meanings and relationships, emotional connections, regimes of bodily inscription, in short, the very stuff of identity and *authority*. Bruce Lincoln nicely describes what such 'authority' is like:

> Ultimately, I want to suggest that discursive authority is not so much an entity as it is ... an effect ... I take the effect to be the result of the conjuncture of the right speaker, the right speech and delivery, the right staging and props, the right time and place, and an audience whose historically and culturally conditioned expectations establish the parameters of what is judged "right" in all these instances. (Lincoln 1994, 10–11)

The religious quality of human bombing consists in just such a 'right' combination of features. These are qualities that lend an *auctoritas* to the act by locating it in a privileged location within this nexus of religious, social, cultural, and affective space. Here the 'power' of the human bomber resides not in the destructive violence of their attacks – not solely in the *potestas* of their military efforts as jihadis. It resides in their becoming 'heroes.' Instead, the 'power' of human bombers in the Middle East derives from their special *auctoritas* as sacrifices understood from a certain – albeit, extreme – Muslim point of view. The religious 'power' of human bombings, understood as sacrifices, lies in their ability to create 'heroes' – to unleash the dynamogenic forces that inspire social flourishing, that reaffirm or create identity, that establish codes of bodily inscription and tap into networks of emotional connection. Beliefs, doctrines, and the rest of the cognitivist set with which religion has usually been identified are still there in some measure. But, as I am in the process of showing, there is so much more, and more that helps us gain a critical understanding of human bombing in the Middle East, than reference to a list of doctrines believed to be true. What is more, I trust that now readers will see how religion can engage politics in ways typically obscured by focusing on clichéd notions of religion as a set of beliefs, or religion as 'good', or religion as alienated from the public and political realms resplendent in its autonomous world of the 'spirit.' It is in the act of sacrifice that my 'interrogated' sense of 'religion' comes into its own.

11. How and Why Sacrifice Works: The Authority of Sacralization

It is one thing to claim that human bomber sacrifice is an embodied projection of *auctoritas,* but quite another thing to say how and why a self-inflicted death can be powerful in this way. There are at least two reasons why such sacrifice projects *auctoritas* – two reasons why human bombers are able to 'add' to the community even when they literally 'subtract' themselves from it. By speaking of 'addition by subtraction,' I am saying that sacrifice causes certain effects in society – it authorizes conceptions of an ideal community, it energizes a society to flourish, it inspires it to resist extermination, it weaves the networks of obligation that make societies cohere. But how does this kind of work get done? I think there are two mechanisms at play here – sacralization and gift exchange.

First, sacralization. Sacrifice works because in giving-up themselves, the human bombers become sacred or holy for their communities. Sacrifice is a kind of ritual machine for manufacturing the sacred. The Latin origins of the term *sacri-ficium* indicate as much; the root meaning of the word 'sacrifice' is 'making holy.' It is essential to this giving-up that it is not, of course, a mere suicide, nor even less part of some utilitarian scheme of truck-and-barter or jihadi projection of *potestas*. The giving of the life of the human bomber enters into the space of the religio-political imaginary: the human bomber is seen as ascending to heaven to be received by Allah. (Lawrence 2005) As the words of Reham, the candidate human bomber, indicate, in death, the human bomber also imagines giving of herself to a non-existent, and thus "imagined community," in Benedict Anderson's sense. "'We know',", says Reham "'what Palestine needs from us'." (Anderson 1991; Jordan 2002) As 'sacred' or 'holy,' the human bombers, like all heroes, rise to a level of transcendent prestige and thus embody a set of values for their communities. They are then paradoxically not *given* at all, but retained by the community, or in the words of Halbwachs, *"embraced"* by the society for whom they die. As sacred, they become preeminent symbolic bearers of the kinds of values that a society treasures as fundamental to it, because as Marxist anthropologist Maurice Godelier observes, they are not part of the normal system of utilitarian truck-and-barter. (Godelier 1999, 32) Instead, they are what society must "conserve, preserve and increase." (Godelier 1999, 35) Sacrifice works in the first sense because the forces thus liberated by actualizing the sacred inform people with strong values. In Israel/Palestine, human bombers are elevated beyond the status of ordinary profane humanity. In the eyes of the community, those who sacrifice themselves for the community rise to the lofty *religious* level of 'martyr.' Raphael Israeli notes that the notorious videos produced before the bombing are devised to provide education and the image of role models for further human bombers; they are far from being like the typical self-pitying or despairing suicide note. (Israeli 1997, 96–112, 105 n. 1) Celebrating one of his 9/11 hijackers, bin Laden shows how the discourse of self-sacrifice, of a total giving-up of one's life, merges with the notion of martyr: "Clear purity and a splendid sacrifice. We beseech Allah to accept him as a martyr." (bin Laden 2001)

By extension, what comes into contact with the sacralized 'victim' itself becomes sacred by contagion. So, not only does sacrifice itself show us religion in embodied form, but so also the fact that sacrifice establishes a 'precinct' or territory of sacrifice adds further embodying features to it. The place of sacrifice becomes itself a sacred place, a place guarded by taboos and withdrawn from ordinary concourse. As the name 'sacri-fice' indicates, while the immolation consists in a gift, it is also at the same time a 'making holy.' So, also, in performing sacrifice for the sake of Palestine, one *ipso facto* 'makes' the bomber holy for Palestinian patriots. At the same time, the sacrifice performed there makes the territory of Palestine 'holy,' since Palestine is a site of an event of making something holy, as well as an intended recipient of sacrifice. One affirms the precincts of its 'holy of holies' – its national borders – as holy by making its territory an arena of sacrifice – much say as the World Trade Center (WTC) site is now generally considered a sacred site, if we are to judge by the persistent invocation of the heroism of the firefighters and police lost in the collapse of the buildings. In this respect, the transformation of the WTC and its site from a quintessentially profane site of commerce into a sacred site of memory and grief is truly a remarkable feat. Observe, as well, that nothing of the same sacredness seems to have adhered to the Pentagon, where, as well, many lives were lost, but no conspicuous acts of sacrifice on the part of rescuers were much noted or perhaps even performed. Perhaps coincidentally, this last intifada bears the name al-Aqsa Intifada, referring to the mosque located within the 66-acre site known to Muslims as the Haram al Sharif ("the Noble Sanctuary") and to Jews as the Har ha-bayit or Temple Mount, both places regarded as holy, although contested, territories. Add to this that the WTC was surely one of the least loved buildings in New York City. Compared to the crystalline elegance of the much-loved Chrysler or Empire State Buildings, the

WTC was an outsized, self-important black slab, projecting crass power onto the Manhattan skyline. That it should now be enshrined in memory and mourned in loss by countless homemade 'shrines' in various media as a tender embodiment of human hopes and dreams, rivals the raising of Lazarus from the dead or the water-to-wine metamorphosis at the wedding feast at Canaan! (Strenski 2002, website).

Whether pretense or not, this intifada, at least in the eyes of some – or at least enough – Palestinians, was provoked by Sharon's visit/intrusion into the sacred place of the Haram al Sharif. Informants in Israel tell me that the Israelis immediately erase any evidence that the sites of Palestinian sacrifice/suicide bombings have ever been the sites of such acts. These sites become, as it were, negative memorials – places of deliberate forgetting – by their rapid return to normal profane uses. Contrast these unmarked – and perhaps unmarkable – sites of the loss of Jewish life to others, such as embodied in the memorial to the Warsaw Ghetto Rising. There the event is embraced with considerable pride, as well, of course, with deep sorrow. (Anon. n.d. c) And compare again the Ghetto Rising memorial to the difficulties afflicting modern representation of the death camps. After so many years, they are still waiting to be comprehended within an appropriate classification at this writing. Are these to be seen as museums, monuments (and to what?), cemeteries? (Webber 1992) If all this be so for Jews, in a future Palestinian state one might well imagine that the very same sites of sacrifice/suicide bombings will become memorials to the bombers who did their sacrificial deeds on what would be, for Palestinians, sacred ground.

Beyond the territory and sacred domain created by sacrifice, those who enable the rite participate in the sacredness created by the sacrificial act. The meager belongings of the 'human bombers' are collected and revered as "relics." Songs are composed about them and their acts, and sung openly in the streets. Their pictures "become the object of worship-like adoration." The families of the human bombers, by a kind of contagion of the sacred, are viewed as "precious in the eyes of the public." They are viewed with "awe and admiration." (Israeli 1997, 96–112, 105–6)

12. How and Why Sacrifice Works: No Free Gifts

The second reason sacrifice works is more complex. Why, first of all, do human bombers bomb, sacrifice themselves – and so do under a sense of obligation? I have already noted that for some Muslims, human bombings as sacrifices are gifts of an extraordinary nature – gifts as a total giving–up, rather than a more restricted giving–of. The author of the single most influential book on gift, Marcel Mauss, argued that gifts are never free, despite what people tend to think about their disinterestedness and spontaneity. Despite the show of pure generosity gift givers typically display, gifts are always given under obligation – the obligations to give, to receive the gift, and to reciprocate. A kind of systematic deception prevails between the appearance of freedom in giving, and its actual restricted nature. In the initial instance, the giver first feels obliged to give – as anyone burdened by the onslaught of Christmas shopping and its endless obligations can attest. Taking matters a step further beyond the obligation to give, there is, second, the additional obligation to receive or accept the gift. As the burdens of holiday shopping should recall, the obligation to accept or receive the gift can be quite oppressive. And, topping both these first two obligations is a third, perhaps even more strongly felt, namely, the obligation to reciprocate, to give in return.

Thus, as gifts, human bombers feel that they are duty-bound to sacrifice themselves – they are giving–up themselves under an obligation. Sacrifice and gift can thus be connected in Islamic traditions, and thus one can interpret the attempted sacrifice of Ishmael as some sort of *hadiyya* or gift. (Ali 2008, pers. comm.) Further, the forms in which the community supports the 'human bombers' draws on a variety of standardized, local religious models. Muslim theology also supports the idea that we owe our lives to Allah, and thus that it is natural to think of sacrificing them to Him. The sense that one does not own oneself, and consequently that one owes oneself to someone else – Allah in particular – is deeply rooted in Islam. Thus, in sacrificing oneself, one admits that Allah has always owned one, and thus self-sacrifice is simply returning to Allah what really belongs to Him. It is what one *ought* to do. Thus, in the Quran (Surah 2, verse 156) it says that "We come and are owned by God, and we all will return to Him." So, self-sacrifice is nothing but a return to Allah of what is His by right. (Ali 2008, pers. comm.) So, in giving-up their lives, the human bombers, in effect, acknowledge this obligation.

But, for human bombers, or any other Muslim for that matter, it is theologically impossible to put Allah under any sort of obligation at all. Allah is Allah after all, and cannot be compelled to do what mere creatures want. That is why one constantly hears in statements praising human bombers by, say Osama bin Laden, the petition that the human bombers be accepted into Allah's graces. "These people," referring to his fighters, says Osama bin Laden, "fought the great unbelief with their hands and their souls, and *we pray to God to accept them as martyrs.*" (My emphasis; Lawrence 2005, 155) Who or what, then, one may ask, can be placed under obligation by the sacrificial gift of the life of a human bomber?

The answer is that the human bombers seek to put the entire community under an obligation. In fact a dual obligation! The human bombers seek to have the community both to feel *obliged* to accept the gift of their deaths and, most importantly, to be *obliged* to repay this gift of their heroic deaths in some appropriate way. Sacrifice works in the second sense, then, because people are constrained to act in certain ways by their situation in an entire network of mutual obligation. Sandra Jordan's 2002 interview with a Palestinian woman and potential human bomber, Reham, again tells us a lot on this score. (Jordan 2002) Entitled "The women who would die for Allah," Jordan shows how Reham speaks a complex religio-political dialect that associates jihad, sacrifice, gift, and martyrdom. What I seek to underline, however, is the tone of *obligation* that persists throughout. Reham is clear, for example, that the sacrifice of her life as a human bomber is a gift – but notably one made under obligation, and to Palestine. Moreover, Reham is well prepared to give Palestine what it "needs," saying clearly that "Everyone should choose sacrifice until we restore our rights." Her concept, then, of sacrifice as gift is fraught with a sense of obligations, as the 'should' and the 'need' of her words indicate. But there is one thing more in Reham's words. Of fighting for Palestine, as a human bomber, she declares: "'It's what I've always wanted to do.'" For her, then, Palestine is a shining ideal, an inspiration that draws her 'forward' to act – as much as a sense of obligation presses upon her 'from behind' to do so as well. And, even though such a 'thing' as Palestine does not yet exist, except in the imagination, this ideal reality draws her into committed action. "'We know what Palestine needs from us','" said Reham.

13. Concluding Remarks

I have intended this example of human bombing in the Middle East as a way to test interrogated notions of religion, power, and politics, and see where they might lead. In that vein, I have noted that although "human bombers" in the Middle East *'look'* like pure projections of potestas, they cannot only be *'seen'* as projections of some imagined autonomous political 'power.' Rather, while they *'look'* to be just political projections of the coercive force of sheer potestas, human bombings in the Middle East also demand to be *'seen'* as 'religious' – as, often self-declared, agents of an ultimate transcendent authority. Along with being jihad, which has its own religious story to tell, the human bombings are to be *'seen'* as projections of an authority – *auctoritas* – rooted in a religious tradition of long – if contested – standing. In order to give them their due, they need to be *'seen'* as ritual sacrifices, as particular sorts of discursive practices articulating a certain vision.

As such, they are not simply 'political' acts, nor are they obviously autonomous of 'religion' in a variety of senses. Nor does their religious quality require them to declare independence of 'power' and 'politics.' These acts create murderous hero-saints, venerated by their communities, sanctified in memory. They sacralize a territory as a venue of sacrifice. They deploy their own authority, and link this to religion in the everyday sense by expressing themselves in the idioms and theologies of well-established, though contested, Islamic traditions. Indeed, while such human bombings might theoretically be carried out as purely autonomous acts of *potestas,* in fact, they are not. While the authority to which they lay hold might as well be only that calling forth political obedience and respect, their authority goes much further and seizes the territory of ultimate commitment and the sacred. With a dark sincerity that cannot be doubted, they not only demand religious authorization – *auctoritas* – but in being what they are, manufacture their own religio-political authority as well.

Human bombings in the Middle East manufacture such religious authority through their individual will and through their community recognition as special kinds of sacrificial gifts. In being sacrificial gifts, they bind the entire community and the human bombers themselves into networks of ultimate obligation. These networks are characterized as religious in invoking and releasing the sacred as they pertain to classic political notions, such as sovereignty and statehood. For the human bombers, sacrality and sovereignty, as we have seen with Palestine, are inextricably married to one another. The "triumph," as well as the achievement of a "secular immortality" of which Asad speaks, only becomes real, then, in terms of a concrete territory and an "imagined community" that seeks to attain the reality of statehood. (Asad 2007, 47, 49) One cannot escape the observation here that the religious element in human bombings in the Middle East enters human affairs not as bloodless creed or a set of beliefs, but as a lived, emotionally connected, bodily inscribed action that creates and projects religious authority even as it attempts to exercise political power.

Here, then, religion engages power, and together they engage in a common effort at a politics. This is not the politics of everyday life, of Foucaultian regimes of interpersonal or non-State domination. This is not the politics that is 'everywhere,' but the politics that congeals about concrete human communities and polities. This is politics in the full-blooded sense that bespeaks a body politic, and indeed a State, or at least, the promise of one. But, in connection with this 'State,' there is no pretense of some sort of 'separation of Church and State.' Neither is there any pretense of an autonomous politics or an autonomous religion. In the case of human bombings in the Middle East, we meet, instead, a situation sharing more in common with the condition of religion and politics in the Christian Middle Ages than with our distinctive modern notions of the separation of religion and politics. So, it is best to lay aside what we take for granted and commonplace about religion and politics, and adapt our conceptualizations to the situation at hand.

It was by confronting such facts that I adapted a strategy toward defining 'religion' in the case explored in this chapter. Given the facts of the situation, I, first, found it implausible to make sense of human bombing without any reference to Islam. But in what sense was Islam involved? Surely, not in the crass ways the Islamophobes of the mass media and their kin see it. We observed how Islamic tradition did not sanction human bombing in any straightforward way. The consensus reading of the story of the attempted sacrifice of Ishmael by Ibrahim, for example, gave no such license to human bombing. The proscription against suicide in Islam is virtually identical to that in the other Abrahamic traditions. On the other hand, I could not *'see'* human bombers in the Middle East as unconnected to traditions peculiar to Islam. The use of Islamic idioms of conception and interpretation did make a kind of Islamic sense.

As I explored what the agents themselves said, what the community surrounding them believed, and what the historical depth of their situation was, it was clear that the 'religion' in human bombing could not be *'seen'* in terms of 'religion' as conceived by the way most of us in the West think about religion – in terms of the six *clichés* I indicted in Chapter 2. Whatever definition of 'religion' obtained in these conventional six senses, it could not stand. 'Religion' needed to be reformed and expanded to take into consideration what we meet today in the Middle East, just as it did in Durkheim's time with the 'discovery' of Theravāda Buddhism by the modern West. Human bombing in the Middle East demanded its own way of nuancing a definition of 'religion.' I judged that there was no better way of getting hold of missing elements of this phenomenon than by recourse to a notion – revised though it may be – of 'religion.' If, then, the acts of human bombing in the Middle East were not simply to be *'seen'* as 'politics' acts in the conventional sense, and all we observed about it reeked of sacrifice, sanctification, martyrdom, and such, then why hesitate calling that neglected aspect of human bombing in the Middle East 'religious'?! Offend the taboos of false reverence we have built up round the notion of 'religion,' and *'see'* the thing for what it is. Human bombing in the Middle East in the cases in question was a religious deed, because it was a *ritual* practice of self-sacrifice, not because it was a matter of beliefs. Human bombing in the Middle East was as well a religious matter, not because it deployed doctrines or confessional declarations, nor less because it made quietistic withdrawal into the recesses of the human heart its hallmark. Human bombing in the Middle East was not a religious act because it was 'good' or avoided shows of 'power.' It was religious because it was a public display of dedication, however gruesome and even 'evil' that display may be. To many Muslims, the religious quality of human bombing does not save it from condemnation as 'bad.' Still less was it clear that in their sacrificial mode, human bombers were being *used* by and for political purposes, even though such sacrificial gifts of the self had political implications. Even murder can have its own integrity, especially when murder is *'seen'* as an act of resistance, altruism, and sacrifice.

It would have been easy for a professor of religious studies to look away, and refuse to *'see'* religion in the human bombing in the

Middle East. After all, few people want others to think that they devote their lives to studying something like religion which, if we take Christopher Hitchens' words to heart, has *"poisoned everything."* (Hitchens 2007, #3445, 27) But, in reading what others had written both from the side of those who blamed Islam for everything evil and from the side of those who could see nothing of Islam in this phenomenon, I could no longer *'look'* at human bombing in the Middle East without declaring that I could *'see'* things there others had missed or deliberately chosen to ignore. My eyes had been trained by years of studying things with very dubious moral credentials, such as religious violence, suicide, the Holocaust, racism, gift, sacrifice, anti-Semitism, ritual, myth, and such in the world's religions. I am willing to accept the consequences of having adopted an approach to yet another unsavory religious phenomenon without flinching before the fact that it made a great deal of sense to understand it as a 'religious' phenomenon. I thus declare my strategies and purposes as elements shaping my approach to defining something like religion. 'Religion' might have been nuanced in quite another way had I been back in Sri Lanka poking about Mindfulness meditation centers. Other questions would have been more salient. Other ways of marking what might have best been called a religious element might have been more to the fore than the need to insert an element of transcendent authority. I am thus pleased to admit my own purposes, as much as they are given to me to understand. I shall leave it to readers to judge whether *'seeing'* religion in the context of human bombing in the Middle East in the way that I have really helps them or not – especially the next time demonstrators march in Tehran, or the next Martin Luther King, Jr. leads a march in an American city.

References

Anderson, B. 1991. *Imagined Communities*. London: Verso.

Anon. 1995. "Religion, Definition of." In *The HarperCollins Dictionary of Religion* (ed.) J. Z. Smith. San Francisco: HarperCollins. 893–4.

Anon. 1998. Khutba – Lessons from the story of Ibrahim (AS) 3 April. www.shu.ac.uk/students/union/socs/Islamic/khtba–ibrahim(as).html.

Anon. 2008. Denmark: Papers Reprint Muhammad Cartoon. *New York Times* February 14. Retrieved September 2, 2009 from www.nytimes.com/2008/02/14/world/europe/14briefs-cartoon.html.

Anon. n.d. a. Significance of Eid. The Story of Prophet Ibrahim's attempt to sacrifice his son (*celebration of Eid Al-Adha*). Retrieved September 2, 2009 from www.guidedones.com/metapage/frq/eidadha10.htm.

Anon. n.d. b. Submission: No Sacrifice of Ishmail. "God never Ordered Abraham to sacrifice his son." Retrieved September 2, 2009 from www.submission.org/Ismail.html.

Anon. n.d. c. Warsaw Ghetto. Warsaw (Warszawa) Photo Gallery. Ghetto Memorials. Retrieved September 2, 2009 from www.biega.com/wwa-3.html.

Anon. n.d. d. Building Our Communities Brick By Brick. Retrieved September 2, 2009 from web.youngmuslims.ca/resources/brochures/99-sacrifice.html.

Appleby, R. S. 2002. Visions of Sacrifice. Roots of Terrorism. *The Christian Century* October 17.

Aron, R. 1986. "Macht, Pouvoir, Puissance: Democratic Prose or Demoniacal Poetry?" In *Power* (ed.) S. Lukes. New York: New York University Press. 253–77.

References

Asad, T. 1993. *Genealogies of Religion: Discipline and Reasons of Power in Christianity and Islam*. Baltimore: Johns Hopkins University Press.

Asad, T. 1996. "Modern Power and the Reconfiguration of Religious Traditions: Interview with Saha Mahmood." *SEHR* (27 February) **5**/1: 1–15.

Asad, T. 2001. "Reading a Modern Classic: W. C. Smith's *The Meaning and End of Religion*." *History of Religions* **40**/3: 205–22.

Asad, T. 2003. *Formations of the Secular: Christianity, Islam, Modernity*. Stanford: Stanford University Press.

Asad, T. 2005. "Reflections on Laïcité & the Public Sphere." *Items and Issues* **5**/3: 1–11.

Asad, T. 2007. *On Suicide Bombing*. New York: Columbia University Press.

Berlin, I. 1979. "The Originality of Machiavelli." In *Against the Current* (ed.) I. Berlin. London: Penguin. 25–79.

Bettenson, H. (ed.) 1970. *Documents of the Christian Church*. Oxford: Oxford University Press.

Bin Laden, O. 2001. Various statements.

Blogger. 2008. *Using Religion for Politics*. The McCotter Monitor, April 14. Retrieved September 2, 2009 from http://mccottermonitor. blogspot.com/2008/04/using-religion-for-politics.html.

Bodin, J. 1975. *Colloquium of the Seven about Secrets of the Sublime* (trans.) M. Kuntz. Princeton: Princeton University Press.

Bossy, J. 1985. *Christianity in the West, 1400–1700*. Oxford: Oxford University Press.

Bossy, J. 1991. "Unrethinking the Sixteenth-Century Wars of Religion." In *Belief in History: Innovative Approaches to European and American Religion* (ed.) T. Kselman. Notre Dame: Notre Dame University Press. 267–85.

Braun, W. 2000. "Religion." In *Guide to the Study of Religion* (eds) W. Braun & R. T. McCutcheon. London: Cassell. 3–20.

Bush, G. W. 2001. Address to a Joint Session of Congress and the American People. Washington, DC: White House Office of the Press Secretary.

Celtel, A. 2005. *Categories of the Self: Louis Dumont's Theory of the Individual*. New York: Berghahn Books.

Chidester, D. 1988. *Patterns of Power: Religion and Politics in American Culture*. Englewood Cliffs: Prentice-Hall.

References

Chidester, D. 1996. *Savage Systems: Colonialism and Comparative Religion in Southern Africa*. Bloomington: Indiana University Press.

Cowdrey, H. E. J. 1985. "Martyrdom and the First Crusade." In *Crusade and Settlement* (ed.) P. Edbury. Cardiff: University of Wales. 46–56.

Davis, N. Z. 1975. "The Rites of Violence." In *Society and Culture in Early Modern France*. Stanford: Stanford University Press.

Dawkins, R. 2006. *The God Delusion*. New York: Houghton and Mifflin.

Decker, L. F. B. 2008. Typical Politician. *Los Angeles Times* June 9, Letters, A15.

Dennett, D. 2007. *Breaking the Spell: Religion as a Natural Phenomenon*. London: Penguin.

Douglas, M. 1980. *Evans-Pritchard*. London: Fontana.

Dumont, L. 1975. "'Preface' by Louis Dumont to the French Edition of *The Nuer*." In *Studies in Social Anthropology* (eds) J. Beattie & R. G. Lienhardt. Oxford: Oxford University Press. 328–42.

Dumont, L. 1979. *Homo Hierarchicus* (trans.) L. D. Mark Sainsbury, Basia Gulati. Chicago: University of Chicago Press.

Dumont, L. 1986a. "Genesis, I: The Christian Beginnings: From the Outworldly Individual to the Individual-in-the-World." In *Essays on Individualism: Modern Ideology in Anthropological Perspective* (ed.) L. Dumont. Chicago: University of Chicago Press. 23–59.

Dumont, L. 1986b. "Genesis, II: The Political Category and the State from the 13th Century Onward." In *Essays on Individualism* (ed.) L. Dumont. Chicago: University of Chicago Press. 60–103.

Dvornik, F. 1951. "Emperors, Popes, and General Councils." *Dumbarton Oaks Papers* **6**/1–23.

Eisenstadt, S. N. (ed.) 1968. *Max Weber: On Charisma and Institution Building*. Chicago: University of Chicago Press.

Evangelical, M.o.t. & S. Committee. 2008. *An Evangelical Manifesto: A Declaration of Evangelical Identity and Public Commitment*. May 7. Retrieved September 2, 2009 from http://www.evangelicalmanifesto.com/media/manifesto.htm.

Evans-Pritchard, E. E. 1940. *The Nuer*. Oxford: Oxford University Press.

Figgis, J. N. 1998. *Studies of Political Thought from Gerson to Grotius, 1414–1625*. Bristol, England: Thoemmes Press.

Fitzgerald, T. 1997. "A Critique of 'Religion' as a Cross-Cultural Category." *Method and Theory in the Study of Religion* **9**/2: 91–110.

189

Fitzgerald, T. 2007. *Discourse on Civility and Barbarity*. Oxford: Oxford University Press.

Flori, J. 1991. "Mort et martyre des guerriers vers 1100: L'exemple de la première croisade." *Cahiers de civilisation médiévale* **34**/121–39.

Flori, J. 2001. *La Guerre Sainte: La formation de l'idée de croisade dans l'Occident chrétien*. Paris: Auber.

Foucault, M. 1977a. "Ch 8. The Eye of Power." In *Power/Knowledge: Selected Interviews and Other Writings, 1972–1977* (ed.) C. Gordon. New York: Pantheon. 146–65.

Foucault, M. 1977b. "Ch 10. The History of Sexuality." In *Power/Knowledge: Selected Interviews and Other Writings, 1972–1977* (ed.) C. Gordon. New York: Pantheon. 183–93.

Foucault, M. 1977c. "Ch 7. Powers and Strategies." In *Power/Knowledge: Selected Interviews and Other Writings, 1972–1977* (ed.) C. Gordon. New York: Pantheon. 134–45.

Foucault, M. 1980. "Ch. 5. Two Lectures." In *Power/Knowledge: Selected Interviews and Other Writings 1972–1977* (ed.) C. Gordon. New York: Pantheon.

Foucault, M. 1988. "Technologies of the Self." In *Technologies of the Self* (eds) L. H. Martin, H. Gutman, & P. H. Hutto. Amherst: The University of Massachusetts Press. 16–49.

Frei, C. 2001. *Hans J. Morgenthau: An Intellectual Biography*. Baton Rouge: Louisiana State University Press.

Friedman, R. B. 1990. "On the Concept of Authority in Political Philosophy." In *Authority* (ed.) J. Raz. New York: New York University Press. 56–91.

Gentile, E. 1996. *The Sacralization of Politics in Fascist Italy* (trans.) K. Botsford. Cambridge: Harvard University Press.

Giddens, A. (ed.) 1986. *Durkheim on Politics and the State*. Stanford: Stanford University Press.

Gladstone, W. 1877. "On the Influence of Authority in Matters of Opinion." *The Nineteenth Century* (March) **1**/3–4.

Godelier, M. 1999. *The Enigma of the Gift* (trans.) N. Scott. Chicago: University of Chicago.

Harris, S. 2006. *Letter to a Christian Nation*. New York: Knopf.

Herrin, J. 1987. *The Formation of Christendom*. Princeton: Princeton University Press.

Hitchens, C. 2007. "Defending 'Islamofascism': It's a Valid Term. Here's Why." *Slate* (22 October).

Hitchens, C. 2007. *God Is Not Great*. New York: Twelve.

Holt, M. P. 1995. *The French Wars of Religion, 1562–1629*. Cambridge: Cambridge University Press.

Hubert, H. & M. Mauss. 1968. "Introduction à l'analyse de quelques phénomènes religieux." In *Marcel Mauss, Oeuvres. Volume 1. Les Fonctions sociales du sacré* (ed.) V. Karady. Paris: Éditions du Minuit. 3–39.

Israeli, R. 1997. "Islamikaze and their Significance." *Terrorism and Political Violence* (Autumn) **9**/2: 96–112.

Israeli, R. 2002. "A Manual of Islamic Fundamentalist Terrorism." *Terrorism and Political Violence* **14**/4: 23–40.

Jahanbegloo, R. 2009. Iran's Clash of Mosque vs. State. *Los Angeles Times* June 15, 3.

Jordan, S. 2002. The Women Who Would Die for Allah. *New Statesman* **131**/4570): 32–7.

Kaplan, B. J. 2007. *Divided by Faith: Religious Conflict and the Practice of Toleration in Early Modern Europe*. Cambridge: Harvard University Press.

Kelsay, J. 2002. Suicide Bombers: The 'Just War' Debate, Islamic Style. *The Christian Century* August 14–27: 22–5.

Kennan, G. F. 1952. *American Diplomacy: 1900–1950*. New York: Mentor.

Knox, R. A. 1950. *Enthusiasm: A Chapter in the History of Religion, with Special Reference to the Seventeenth and Eighteenth Centuries*. Oxford: Oxford University Press.

Küng, H. 2007. *The Catholic Church*. New York: Modern Library.

Lawrence, B. (ed.) 2005. *Messages to the World: The Statements of Osama bin Laden*. London: Verso.

Lease, G. 1994. "The History of 'Religious' Consciousness and the Diffusion of Cultural Strategies for Surviving Dissolution." *Historical Reflections/Refléxions Historiques* **20**/453–79.

Lilla, M. 2008. *The Stillborn God*. New York: Vintage.

Lincoln, B. 1994. *Authority: Construction and Corrosion*. Chicago: University of Chicago Press.

Lincoln, B. 2003. *Holy Terrors: Thinking about Religion after September 11*. Chicago: University of Chicago Press.

Lukes, S. 1972. *Emile Durkheim*. New York: Harper and Row.

References

Margalit, A. 2003. The Suicide Bombers. *The New York Review of Books* **50**/1:36–9.

Max. 2001. World: Daily News: ABC News.

McCutcheon, R. T. 2001. *Critics Not Caretakers Redescribing the Public Study of Religion*. Albany: SUNY.

Minogue, K. 1995. *Politics: A Very Short Introduction*. Oxford: Oxford University Press.

Morgenthau, H. J. 1962. "The Influence of Reinhold Niebuhr in American Political Life and Thought." In *Reinhold Niebuhr: A Prophetic Voice of Our Time* (ed.) H. R. Landon. Greenwich, CT: Seabury Press. 97–110.

Morgenthau, H. J. 1965. *Politics among Nations: The Struggle for Power and Peace*. New York: Alfred A. Knopf.

Morris, C. 1989. *The Papal Monarchy: The Western Church from 1050 to 1250*. Oxford: Oxford University Press.

Murphy, K. 2008. Tony Blair details role of his faith. *Los Angeles Times* April 30. Retrieved September 2, 2009 from http://articles.latimes.com/2008/apr/30/world/fg-blair30.

Nelson, B. 1969. *The Idea of Usury: from Tribal Brotherhood to Universal Otherhood*. Chicago: University of Chicago Press.

Neuhaus, R. J. 1984. *The Naked Public Square: Religion and Democracy in America*. Grand Rapids: William B. Eerdmans.

Nogent, G. O. 1997. *The Deeds of God through the Franks* (trans.) R. Levine. Woodbridge, Suffolk: Boydell and Brewer.

Oakley, F. 1962. "On the Road from Constance to 1688: The Political Thought of John Major and George Buchanan." *Journal of British Studies* (March) 1/2: 1–31.

Oakley, F. 1996. "'Anxieties of Influence': Skinner, Figgis and Early Modern Constitutionalism." *Past and Present* **151**/May: 60–110.

Oakley, F. 2003. *The Conciliar Tradition*. Oxford: Oxford University Press.

Oakley, F. 2006. *Kingship*. Oxford: Blackwell.

Obama, B. 2006. *The Audacity of Hope: Thoughts on Reclaiming the American Dream*. New York: Crown.

Orwell, G. 1948. "Appendix: The Principles of Newspeak." In *1984* (ed.) G. Orwell. London: Harcourt Brace. 267–79.

Orwell, G. 1956. "Politics and the English Language." In *The Orwell Reader* (ed.) R. H. Rovere. New York: Harcourt, Brace & World. 355–66.

References

Ozment, S. 1980. *The Age of Reform 1250–1550*. New Haven: Yale University Press.

Pape, R. A. 2003. Dying to Kill Us. *New York Times* September 22. Retrieved September 2, 2009 from www.nytimes.com/2003/09/22/opinion/dying-to-kill-us.html.

Pape, R. A. 2005. *Dying to Win: The Strategic Logic of Suicide Terrorism*. New York: Random House.

Pelikan, J. 2003. *Credo: Historical and Theological Guide to Creeds and Confessions of Faith in the Christian Tradition*. New Haven: Yale University Press.

Peters, R. S. 1958. "Authority." *Proceedings of the Aristotelian Society. Supplementary Volumes* **32**/207–24.

Philpott, D. 2000. "The Religious Roots of Modern International Relations." *World Politics* **52**/2: 206–45.

Pickering, W. S. F. 1984. *Durkheim's Sociology of Religion: Themes and Theories*. London: Routledge.

Polanyi, K. 1944. *The Great Transformation*. New York: Farrar and Rinehart.

Ranulf, S. 1939. "Scholarly Forerunners of Fascism." *Ethics* **50**/16–34.

Raz, J. 1986. *The Morality of Freedom*. Oxford: Oxford University Press.

Réville, A. 1874. "Contemporary Materialism in Religion: the Sacred Heart." *Theological Review* **44**/January: 138–56.

Réville, A. 1905. *Lectures on the Origin and Growth of Religion [1884]* (trans.) P. H. Wicksteed. London: Williams and Norgate.

Réville, J. 1907. "Leçon d'ouverture du cours d'histoire des religions au Collège de France." *Revue de l'histoire des religions* **55**/189–207.

Riley-Smith, L. & J. Riley-Smith. 1981. *The Crusades: Idea and Reality 1095–1274*. London: Edward Arnold.

Rivière, J. 1912. "La redemption devant la pensée moderne." *La revue du clergé français 70* **284**/285, 98, 99.

Robertson, P. 2007. Broadcast of 12 June 2007 (trans.) C. B. Network, USA. In *The 700 Club*. Retrieved September 2, 2009 from http://mediamatters.org/research/200804090011.

Sabatier, A. 1904. *The Doctrine of the Atonement and Its Historical Evolution* (trans.) V. Leuliette. London: Williams and Northgate.

Schmitt, C. 2005a. *The Concept of the Political* (trans.) G. Schwab. Chicago: University of Chicago Press.

Schmitt, C. 2005b. *Political Theology: Four Chapters on the Concept of Sovereignty* (trans.) G. Schwab. Chicago: University of Chicago Press.

Scott, D. 2006. "Appendix The Trouble of Thinking: An Interview with Talal Asad." In *Powers of the Secular Modern: Talal Asad and His Interlocutors* (eds) D. Scott & C. Hirschkind. Stanford: Stanford University Press. 243–303.

Singer, R. 2009. Letter from Robert Singer, responding to Michele Madigan Somerville's "Born Again in Brooklyn." *New York Times* June 27.

Skinner, Q. 1978. *The Foundations of Modern Political Thought. Volume 2: The Age of Reformation.* Cambridge: Cambridge University Press.

Smart, N. 1983. *Worldviews: Crosscultural Explorations of Human Beliefs.* New York: Scribners.

Smith, J.Z. 2004. "Religion, Religions, Religious." In *Relating Religions* (ed.) J. Z. Smith. Chicago: University of Chicago Press. 179–96.

Strenski, I. 1987. *Four Theories of Myth in Twentieth-Century History.* Iowa City: Iowa University Press.

Strenski, I. 1993a. "Henri Hubert, Racial Science and Political Myth." In *Religion in Relation* (ed.) I. Strenski. London: Macmillan. 180–201.

Strenski, I. 1993b. "Love and Anarchy in Romania." In *Religion in Relation* (ed.) I. Strenski. Columbia: University of South Carolina Press. 166–79.

Strenski, I. 1998a. "Durkheim's Bourgeois Theory of Sacrifice." In *On Durkheim's Elementary Forms of the Religious Life* (eds) N. J. Allen, W. S. F. Pickering & W. W. Miller. London: Routledge. 116–26.

Strenski, I. 1998b. "Religion, Power and the Final Foucault." *JAAR* (Summer 1998) **66**/2: 345–68.

Strenski, I. 2002. *Spontaneous Shrines.* Riverside, CA: University of California, Riverside.

Strenski, I. 2003a. "Sacrifice, Gift and the Social Logic of Muslim 'Human Bombers'." *Terrorism and Political Violence* **15**/2: 1–34.

Strenski, I. 2003b. *Theology and the First Theory of Sacrifice.* Leiden: E. J. Brill.

Strong, T. B. 2007. "Foreword." In *Carl Schmitt, The Concept of the Political* (ed.) T. B. Strong. Chicago: University of Chicago Press. ix–xxi.

Taylor, C. 1985a. "Foucault of Freedom and Truth." In *Philosophy and the Human Sciences: Philosophical Papers, 2* (ed.) C. Taylor. Cambridge: Cambridge University Press. 152–84.

Taylor, C. 1985b. "Understanding and Ethnocentricity." In *Philosophy and the Human Sciences: Philosophical Papers, 2* (ed.) C. Taylor. Cambridge: Cambridge University Press. 116–33.

Tiele, C. P. 1898. *Elements of the Science of Religion. Part 2: Ontological.* Edinburgh and London: W. Blackwood and Sons.

Tierney, B. 1964. *The Crisis of Church and State 1050–1300.* Englewood Cliffs: Prentice-Hall.

Urban II, P. 1981. "Four Letters on Crusading from Pope Urban II." In *The Crusades: Idea and Reality 1095–1274* (eds) L. Riley-Smith & J. Riley-Smith. London: Edward Arnold. 37–40.

Volpi, F. & B. S. Turner. 2007. "Introduction. Making Islamic Authority Matter." *Theory, Culture and Society* **24**/1: 1–19.

Walzer, M. 1986. "The Politics of Michel Foucault." In *Foucault: A Critical Reader* (ed.) D. C. Hoy. Oxford: Blackwell. 51–68.

Walzer, M. 1992. *Regicide and Revolution: Speeches at the Trial of Louis XVI.* New York: Columbia University Press.

Watson, J. 1997. *The Christian Coalition: Dreams of Restoration, Demands for Recognition.* New York: St. Martin's.

Webber, J. 1992. *The Future of Auschwitz.* Oxford: Oxford Centre for Postgraduate Hebrew Studies.

Weber, M. 1946. "Politics as a Vocation." In *From Max Weber: Essays in Sociology* (eds) H. H. Gerth & C. W. Mills. New York: Oxford University Press. 77–128.

Wieseltier, L. 1991. "Two Concepts of Secularism." In *Isaiah Berlin: A Celebration* (eds), E. Margalit & A. Margalit. Chicago: University of Chicago Press. 80–99.

Wilson, W. 1913. Inaugural Address. March 4. Retrieved September 2 from www.bartleby.com/124/pres44.html.

Yaseen, S. A. 2002. Eid message to the Ummah from Shaikh Ahmad Yaseen on the Struggle in Palestine. February 19. Retrieved September 2, 2009 from www.yaseenday.com/articles/muslimedia.htm.

Index